A Cambodian Prison Portrait
One Year in
the Khmer Rouge's S-21

A Cambodian Prison Portrait

One Year in the Khmer Rouge's S-21

Vann Nath

Translated by
Moeun Chhean Nariddh

White Lotus Press

In memory
of all the people who suffered and died
as a result of the Khmer Rouge regime.
May they be reborn into a more peaceful world.

White Lotus Co. Ltd.
G.P.O. Box 1141
Bangkok 10501
Thailand

Telephone: (662) 332-4915 and (662) 741-6288-9
Fax: (662) 741-6607 and (662) 741-6287

E-mail: ande@loxinfo.co.th

Webpage: http://thailine.com/lotus

Printed in Thailand

ISBN 974-8434-48-6 pbk White Lotus Co. Ltd., Bangkok

Contents

Foreword

Bringing the memoirs and paintings of Vann Nath to publication had its origin, in part, in coffee breaks that my co-worker Leah Melnick and I used to take in 1993 around the corner from where we worked. There we often met the owner of the coffee shop: a white-haired man with a youthful face, piercing eyes, and gentle voice. Over time as we sat with him in the open-air courtyard of his shop, we learned that his name was Vann Nath and that he was a survivor of Tuol Sleng Prison. A painter by trade, Nath still held vivid images of what he saw, heard, and felt at Tuol Sleng; often grabbing a pencil to sketch a scene for us. Later Leah translated for Chris Riley when he was researching the prison, and it was Chris who first encouraged Nath to put his memories to paper. Moeun Chhean Nariddh and Choeung Pochin translated Nath's writings and interviews from Khmer to English. As the writing began to take shape in English, others helped out with editing and proofreading: Tom McCarthy, Doug Niven, Andy Maxwell, Peter Eng, and David Chandler. Photographs were provided by Martin Flitman, Andy Maxwell, David ven der Veen, and Darren Whiteside.

Sara Colm
Phnom Penh
April 1998

Further Reading

Becker, Elizabeth. *When the War was Over: The Voices of Cambodia's Revolution and Its People*. New York: Simon and Schuster, 1986.

Caldwell, Malcolm and Lek Tan. *Cambodia in the Southeast Asian War*. New York: Monthly Review Press, 1973.

Chandler, David. *Brother Number One: A Political Biography of Pol Pot*. Boulder: Westview Press, 1992.

_____. *The Tragedy of Cambodian History*. New Haven: Yale University Press, 1991.

Evans, Grant and Kelvin Rowley. *Red Brotherhood at War: Indochina Since the Fall of Saigon*. London: Verso Editions, 1984.

Heder, Stephen. "Kampuchea's Armed Struggle: The Origins of an Independent Revolution." *Bulletin of Concerned Asian Scholars*, Vol. II, No. 1 (Jan.-March 1979).

Jackson, Karl, Ed. *Cambodia 1975-1978: Rendezvous with Death*. Princeton: Princeton University Press, 1989.

Kiernan, Ben. *How Pol Pot Came to Power*. London: Verso, 1985.

_____. *The Pol Pot Regime: Race, Power and Genocide in Cambodia under the Khmer Rouge, 1975-79*. New Haven: Yale University Press, 1996.

Kiljunen, Kimmo, Ed. *Kampuchea: Decade of the Genocide: Report of a Finnish Inquiry Commission*. London: Zed Books Ltd., 1984.

Martin, Marie. *Cambodia: A Shattered Society*. Berkeley: University of California Press, 1994.

Meyer, Charles. *Derrière le Sourire Khmer*. Paris: Plon, 1971

Riley, Chris and Doug Niven, Eds, with text by Vann Nath, David Chandler, and Sara Colm. *The Killing Fields*. Twin Palms Press, 1996.

Shawcross, William. *Sideshow: Kissinger, Nixon and the Destruction of Cambodia*. New York: Simon and Schuster, Inc., 1987.

Thion, Serge. *Watching Cambodia*. Bangkok: White Lotus Press, 1993.

Vickery, Michael. *Cambodia: 1975-1982*. Boston: South End Press, 1984.

Introduction

During the Khmer Rouge regime in Cambodia from April 1975 to January 1979, a former high school in Phnom Penh known as Tuol Sleng was converted into a prison called S-21. More than 14,000 men, women and children passed through the gates of S-21 before being executed by the Khmer Rouge, their bodies dumped at Choeung Ek on the outskirts of town.

During their three years, eight months and 20 days in power, the Khmer Rouge declared 200,000 Cambodians enemies of the state and executed them. Hundreds of thousands more died of starvation, overwork, or disease. The total death toll is estimated at more than one million.

I was one of only seven inmates in S-21 who escaped execution. Even though Cambodia's tragedy of the 1970s has passed, the memories are fresh in my mind.

Nowadays, when I visit Tuol Sleng, I am overcome by this painful past. Everything that happened to me comes flooding back: the terror and shock, the ghost-like emaciated people, the screams of pain echoing through the prison, the brutality of the prison guards. The pale faces of the prisoners seem to look at me from every corner, crying, "Help! Please help me..."

I never expected to survive this hell. I spent exactly one year in S-21. On January 7, 1978 I was thrust there not knowing why I was arrested. On January 7, 1979, I escaped.

My story is surreal, a bizarre tale of millions of people massacred by their own government without hesitation or judgment. As for those who escaped death, they were deprived of all rights and even emotions, sculpted to serve as the tools of the rulers. When Cambodia's doors reopened again in 1979, little remained but tears and piles of bones. Today the blood has dried up but the scars remain. The legacy of the Khmer Rouge regime lives on today — in the separated families, the orphans, the thousands of haunted, wounded people. The chief criminals and their henchmen who were responsible for the atrocities still live comfortably and safely; nobody dares touch them.

This book is dedicated to all who perished in Tuol Sleng. By keeping their memory alive, my hope is that their deaths do not lose all meaning but can help a new generation of Cambodians, and people throughout the world, to understand what happened in my motherland in the 1970s.

—**Vann Nath**

Peace Time

I was born into a farming family in 1946. Our home was in Battambang, a city in northwestern Cambodia 300 kilometers from the capital of Phnom Penh. Before the 1970 war, Battambang was a peaceful province, known as the country's rice bowl because the land was so fertile. The people were generally well off and did not experience hunger.

After several years in the monkhood as a teenager, I chose painting as my profession, which had been my favorite subject since childhood. I studied with a private teacher for a while, then took up an apprenticeship with another artist. Because I had talent I learned quickly and in 1969 I opened a small business with several partners. We painted cinema placards, private portraits, and huge billboards of King Sihanouk to welcome his entourage when he visited Battambang. Although my income was not very high, I was satisfied with my career and was able to provide a modest living for my family.

On March 18, 1970, General Lon Nol staged a coup to overthrow the monarchy. War blazed throughout the country and power was grabbed by armed men. The new government conscripted young men all over Cambodia; no one could escape. One faction — the Khmer Rouge — hid in the forest, while the other stayed inside the halls of power, headquartered in Phnom Penh. The two sides brutally confronted each other and used innocent people as their pawns.

The Khmer Rouge tried to mobilize the people in the rural areas, and indoctrinate them in Maoist ideology. They said that those in power were the puppets of "American imperialists." Under Khmer Rouge control the people were forced to abandon private property and had to farm collectively. The government countered with its own propaganda. They challenged people to join the army to defend the country, which they said had been invaded by the Vietnamese, the "Yuons." What was the true story?

The Chaos Begins

It was April 13, 1975. I did not go to work because it was the Khmer New Year. But for me the holiday meant nothing. Battambang's streets were jammed with people from the rural areas taking refuge from the war in the city's monasteries and schools. In the hospitals, wounded people spilled out of the rooms and onto the hallways, while armed men wandered around menacingly. Artillery pounded the outskirts of town, which meant that the Red Army had surrounded Battambang, defeating "the imperialists."

It was widely known that General Lon Nol and a number of high-ranking commanders had fled Phnom Penh, and that the American Embassy had withdrawn as well. Still, many of us thought peace negotiations would take place between the two factions.

On New Year's day my wife and I took some food to the pagoda to offer to the monks to pray for happiness. To my surprise, I found more than ten coffins there with a photograph placed in front of each. At one side the families of the dead were crying. I saw the picture of a man who was an acquaintance of mine and rushed to his family to find out what had happened. The brother of the dead man took my hand.

"Brother, what happened?" I asked him. "I just met my friend a few days ago."

"That's right," the man replied with a dark look. "Three days ago, he was on guard in O Dambang village. Yesterday, the Khmer Rouge launched a big attack and many people were killed — both soldiers and militiamen. They still have not removed all the bodies. My brother was seriously wounded and died at the hospital last night."

I sighed deeply to relieve the tension in my heart. After lighting incense sticks to commemorate the spirit of the dead, I went to offer food to the monks. Oh God, more people have died, I thought.

That night I lay anxiously listening to the sound of artillery coming from all directions. This time last year, the streets were crowded with villagers playing traditional games, cheering and shouting happily. While we had an 8 p.m. curfew, during the New Year it was lifted until midnight. But this year everything was quiet except the big guns. And while New Year was usually a time for making trips to visit relatives, this year the war made it dangerous to travel even one kilometer from home.

I had been praying for immediate negotiations to bring peace. Living in the fire of war was like living on a planet with no sun. The strong could do anything to the weak whenever they wanted to. It was difficult for me to earn money because as a militia man I was frequently called to stand guard in different places. I could pay a bribe if I didn't want to go, but where could I get the money? So I always had to show up for guard duty, using my chest to prevent bullets from hitting the rich.

Three days passed and the New Year was over. I rode my bicycle to my painting shop to see if there was any work for me to do. I found the doors wide open. My fellow workers and teacher were sitting there, chatting happily. They laughed and smiled at me, saying, "The war is over now!"

"Really, brothers! How do you know?" I asked.

"They have reached agreement during their talks," one of the workers replied. "At the airport, they shook hands with soldiers from the liberating army."

I was very pleased and headed home to tell my family the good news. But as I bent my back to cycle up the new concrete bridge over the Sangkhe River towards my home, the sound of gunfire burst out in front of me. I put on the brakes and looked around. At the eastern end of the bridge I spotted about 20 men in the black uniforms of the Khmer Rouge carrying guns. The gunfire had scattered other pedestrians. Some were running across the bridge, while others were running towards me.

I got off my bicycle and walked it slowly forwards. I asked people who were running what happened, but nobody answered. They all looked pale and some were pulling along bicycles or motorbikes. At the end of the bridge, I found a body lying in a puddle of blood in the middle of the road. It was a couple of moments before I realized that one of the black-uniformed men was calling me.

"Hey, that comrade who is walking a bicycle! Where are you going?" he yelled.

"Yes, brothers, I am going home from work," I replied in a shaky voice.

"What is your job?" he shouted.

"I am a painter," I answered, taking a quick glance at the corpse, which was dressed in the uniform of a government soldier.

"Don't be afraid," he said. "This is just to warn some stubborn prisoners of war."

At the same time, another man carrying an AK-47 rifle carefully pointed it at me. My hair stood on end.

"Do you have a gun?" he asked.

"No, I don't, Brother!" I replied, raising my hands for him to search me.

A pile of guns and ammunition lay on the ground nearby. After searching me, the soldiers allowed me to proceed. There were no vehicles on the bridge and I quickly walked my bicycle away. After about 20 meters, I got on the bike and sped homeward without looking back. As I rode I guessed that the dead soldier might have refused to hand over his weapon. But why did they kill people like animals? Full of fear, I arrived home before I realized it. My neighbors were in the street, gathered around a radio which was broadcasting loudly: "We are the winners this time. Not because of negotiations, but because of weapons. Therefore, all the puppet soldiers must quietly lay down your weapons and bow your heads to surrender. If not, *Angkar* will not forgive you!"

The term "Angkar" was something I was to hear repeatedly over the next several years. It referred to the faceless and nameless leaders of the Khmer Rouge.

The radio broadcast the same thing over and over. I wasn't sure then about what my friends had said that morning — that the factions had reached agreement in their talks. That afternoon I did not return to work for fear of a repetition of the morning's events. Late in the day black-uniformed soldiers carrying weapons appeared all over the village, walking in groups of four or five. The villagers were friendly to them and gave them cakes to eat. Some villagers condemned the Lon Nol government, saying it was corrupt. I didn't dare talk with these men in black because the morning's events were still on my mind.

Night fell. The artillery was silent now, replaced instead by the sporadic sound of small arms fire rattling around the city. Hearing the shooting, I pictured people being killed like the man shot by the bridge that morning. Late into the night I could hear people walking across the village, making the dogs bark. I closed my eyes and prayed for the dawn to come soon so that I could find out what was happening.

The morning of April 18th arrived but I did not go to work. Instead my wife and I went to her sister's house to get some news. We passed through the center of town: the doors of all the shops were shut although food, cakes, and drink were set in front of each house to welcome the new army. In the market, people were pushing each other at the stalls to buy food. Unsure of what was happening, I stopped my bicycle and asked around. People said our army friends had fixed the prices of goods for people to sell. Yesterday, the price of pork was 5,000 riel per kilo, but today it was lowered to only 100 riel. Everyone was very happy! The price of rice had also gone down.

We did not dare enter the market as there were too many people there. Instead we went straight to my sister-in-law's house west of the market. When we went upstairs, my sister-in-law looked as if nothing had happened. She smiled broadly at us. "Our country has peace now," she said. "At the market, the prices of all kinds of goods have all gone down."

I shared this pleasure with her, but asked: "Sister, they said they had reached an agreement with each other and ended the war. But why did the radio announcer order the soldiers to lay down their weapons? I don't quite understand."

Before she could answer, horns blared out along the street in front of her house. A truck with black-uniformed soldiers riding on the roof clutching guns passed by, broadcasting for all soldiers to lay down their weapons and report to designated areas. Officers were to go to Komarey Sor Heu Primary School and the enlisted men were to report to Monivong School.

"This is very strange," I said to my sister-in-law.

"I don't know — let's wait for your brother to return from work to get more news," she said as I followed her back into the house.

When my brother arrived at 11:30 we asked him what was happening.

"Colonel Tan Pok, the doctor at Military Hospital 403, was taken to be killed last night along with ten other colleagues," he said, his face showing no emotion.

Killing doctors? This made no sense. I asked my brother if he had heard the trucks ordering the government soldiers to gather at schools. "Maybe they are gathering them to kill them," I said.

My brother replied without thinking much. "It can't be like that! Maybe they are taking them to go and study their new laws. This morning, I saw a few high-ranking officers riding in the same trucks with those men. They were dressed in black clothes with red checked *krahma* scarves hanging around their necks. As far as I know, there won't be a big problem."

He paused and then said: "But there was one interesting thing this morning. When some hospital staff rode their motorcycles to work, they were stopped by those comrades who demanded the motorcycles from them. Some even had their wrist watches taken away. If anyone dared to protest, they would..."

"They would be killed, wouldn't they, Brother?" I said.

"Maybe," he replied, looking into my eyes.

I told him everything I had seen since the previous day. His expression changed several times and afterwards he was quiet for awhile. Then he surprised me by telling me the provincial governor had fled yesterday, escaping through Pailin with a battalion of soldiers and ten tanks.

Oh God, was that our so-called patriotic governor, who had always considered himself a hero? An entourage of guards accompanied him in his escape, but he wouldn't care how many people died to protect his life. The guards would be abandoned once he arrived in Thailand. Later, if he had a chance, he would return and become a big man again.

After lunch, my wife and I went back home. On our way past the bridge where the government soldier lay dead, the black-clad soldiers were still collecting weapons. The pile of guns was higher but the traffic flowed normally. The sound trucks continued to blare their message up and down the streets: all soldiers must report to the schools immediately. Along the way home, I saw twice as many black-uniformed soldiers carrying guns. Some of them were only about 13 or 14 years old, but their behavior was menacing all the same.

Many soldiers from my village went to report at the schools. I saw them preparing themselves by putting on their uniforms and leaving the village one by one. Some had already left the army more than a year before, but they still went along with other soldiers. I worried about my own situation because I used to take a shift guarding the village nearly every week. But almost everyone in the village, except children, was entrusted with that duty.

That evening my village was noisier than usual. Every house cooked food to present to the black-uniformed soldiers. Some of my neighbors were chatting in a friendly manner with those comrades who looked friendly. But I did not dare go near them. One neighbor whispered softly to me: "You know, last night all the commune chiefs were taken to be killed in the rice field behind the village. Their bodies are still there. Their wives did not dare to go near."

His words frightened me. "We've heard only 'kill! kill!' so far," I said. "And the governor and his group have all fled."

"Don't worry too much," my friend responded. "We are the poor people. Nobody will take us away."

Separation

It was April 20. The previous day I had not gone out but stayed quietly at home hoping to get some news on the radio. But the programs were nothing but revolutionary music and announcements for government soldiers to lay down their weapons and surrender. Despite protests from my wife, I decided to go and check on my painting shop. I had not been there for a couple of days.

Along the streets, things did not seem out of the ordinary. I crossed the bridge and pedaled my bike by the school where they had gathered the soldiers. It was dead quiet there and all the soldiers were gone. As I passed by I saw a friend walking very fast in the opposite direction. I stopped my bicycle and called to him.

"Hey, Soeung! Where are you going so fast?"

He turned and walked towards me, looking very pale.

"My dad was told to report here but he was taken away last night in a truck," Soeung told me, his voice shaking. "They said they went to receive the King. He told me to bring him his badges and clothes. I saw him dressed up nicely with the badges of a major handsomely attached to his shoulders as he got into the truck with many of his friends. But then I was told that they were all taken to be killed."

"Don't believe such nonsense!" I said. "Who told you?"

"My friend. He knows this for sure because his cousin's brother is one of the liberation soldiers."

"So where are you going now?" I asked. He seemed very panicked.

"I want to ask those soldiers who are on guard at that school whether it is true."

"You're crazy, Soeung. You must definitely not go there!" I said. "If you go and ask them, you are telling them that you are a son of a major. So, don't!"

I persuaded Soeung to return home. Once he headed off I felt even more tense. Was what he had told me true or just rumor? My thoughts were chaotic as I pedaled to the painting shop. The doors were slightly ajar but no one was there except the house owner.

"Brother, have the other painters come these last few days?" I asked.

"Nobody came to work," he said. "They just stopped in for a brief look."

As we sat down for a chat suddenly we heard a loudspeaker outside.

"*Angkar* orders all the people to leave the city at once ... If any comrades refuse to leave, they must be responsible for themselves."

We stopped talking and rushed out to hear the announcement more clearly. A jeep with a loudspeaker mounted on it was passing by slowly. Many groups of the black-uniformed soldiers walked on both sides of the pavement, yelling harshly at the people. I realized that the chaos had come. I pulled out my bicycle and waved goodbye to the house owner.

"You don't need to take too much along with you!" the voice said over the loudspeaker. "*Angkar* only asks you to leave for three days. Quick! Quick! The Americans will drop bombs very soon!"

The threats were accompanied by gunfire to force people out of their houses and hustle them down the streets. I ran with my bicycle to my sister-in-law's house. When I arrived, her husband was loading luggage onto a cart. Their children were crying.

"Brother, where are you going?" I asked.

"We were told to leave the city for three days," he said.

"Where will you go?" I asked.

"We're not sure. We'll try to wait for the others."

I said a quick goodbye to my relatives and rushed home. My house was about three kilometers away from the market — and I had to cross the bridge again.

The streets were full of anarchy and disorder. Some people were carrying luggage on their heads or shoulders. Others were carrying their crying children. Some parents had lost their children while children wandered about screaming for their parents. Gunshots rang through the streets.

I pushed through the crowds of people, racing to catch up with my wife and children. As I began to walk my bike across the bridge, black-uniformed men on the other side suddenly began to shoot into the air, forcing everyone off the bridge. With the bridge now closed, I knew it would be useless to beg them. I turned my bike backwards to the left and went along the riverside to the north; I could also reach my home that way. The problem was that I would have to swim across the river.

Along the way, soldiers stopped me many times but each time I lied to them that my house was not far off. At the ferry port where boats usually carried people across the river, no boats were in sight. I leaned my bike again a tree, took off my clothes and swam across the river. I was dead tired and could hardly reach the bank. I ran the rest of the way to my village. Some people were still moving luggage into their carts but I found my house empty. All of our belongings were still there — but where was my wife? I ran to ask my neighbors.

"Aunt, do you know where my wife went?" I asked.

"I saw her holding your child and heading south. She said she was going to her sister's house."

I ran to the river and swam back across, fearing I had missed my wife on the way. On the other side I could not find my bicycle. The streets were blocked by crowds of people so I zigzagged left and right to get through. Finally I arrived at my sister-in-law's house but it was too late. Everyone was already gone, leaving only a quiet house. I had no energy left in my body. The people living next door had not all left yet. I rushed around frantically asking where my family had gone but nobody knew. Finally I could not think what else to do so I pushed ahead, following the crowds of people to the west. The black-uniformed soldiers continued firing into the air to threaten everyone to move along. If anyone dared to turn back, the soldiers pointed guns at their heads.

Exodus

I had nothing but the clothes on my back. It was late in the afternoon and the soldiers began to force the people along even more brutally. When they first arrived several days earlier, they called people "Dad and Mom," and said: "Your children have come to liberate Dad and Mom from the imperialists, from the suppression of the feudalists." Now they were really liberating: they liberated people out of the city, pushing them out of their homes by force.

I walked like a soulless man, my eyes darting around looking for my family. I was angry with myself for leaving the house and leaving my family alone. Nobody could have known such a thing would happen but that did not make me feel better about it. I had lost my family. In only two or three hours the soldiers had moved all the people out. The entire town of Battambang turned silent.

It was now five o'clock. I walked to Chamkar Chek village, about five kilometers from the city, and collapsed on the pavement in despair. They were not pushing along the people too strongly then, and others were also stopping to recover their strength. The black-uniformed soldiers were walking in groups to inspect the situation. I turned to the left and to the right many times, looking for my family and not knowing what to do. Finally, I found a painter friend of mine. He was luckier than me, because he had his whole family with him. They were even able to bring along some rice and cooking pots.

His name was Than. We had worked together for almost a year. He persuaded me to join his family for the journey because I didn't have any food. The soldiers ordered everyone to cook their meals and rest in Chamkar Chek.

"If anyone doesn't have any food, *make contact* with each other," they said, using strange jargon that I had never heard before. I did not understand what they meant but I didn't care very much.

After the meal, night came. I asked Than to walk around with me to try to get some news about my family. But it was too dark to see people's faces clearly and we could not go very far because guards were everywhere.

One day, two days passed and people moved slowly along the highway toward Thmar Kaul village. The people there had not yet been moved. The people from Battambang were told to get off the national highway. Some went north, while others headed south. My friend and I turned south.

After finding a good place to camp, we decided to temporarily settle there. Luckily, I met a former neighbor who said he had seen my wife at the provincial hospital on the day Battambang was evacuated. My wife had also asked about me but no one knew where I was then, he said. That was all he knew. After hearing this news, I felt re-energized, more hopeful than I had in days.

That night, I sat up alone looking at the sky and stars overhead. I was determined to get more news about my wife the next day. In the distance, the sound of trucks coming and going several kilometers away went on throughout the night. What were they doing that time of the night? I went to talk to Than.

"Maybe *Angkar* is taking rice to give to us?" Than said.

His thinking made sense, because we had only received one tin of rice during the last ten days.

The next morning I got up unusually early, feeling fresher than I had felt since leaving Battambang, and set off to another village about 13 kilometers south. Along the way, there were people coming and going endlessly. The soldiers were not so strict now about where people moved as long as they stayed away from the city. I hoped to trade a watch I had hidden from the soldiers for some rice. My remaining Lon Nol money — about 10,000 riels — was worthless.

Along the way I heard someone calling my name from a shabby lean-to. It was one of my oldest friends. Before I could ask him anything, he said: "Nath, did you find your wife yet? Three or four trucks came in last night from Ta Ngen. Go look for her."

I ran and walked very fast for six or seven kilometers without feeling tired. At the village, I looked around and, finally I found my wife. All the pain hidden in my chest for over a week burst out as tears. I could not say anything for a moment and embraced my wife and child tightly in my arms.

She told me that an hour after I had left home, soldiers fired into the air and ordered everyone to move out. My wife had only a couple of minutes to grab a small bundle of clothes. They took a boat to the western bank of the river where they met my oldest brother, who was a doctor. They stayed the next five days at the hospital with him, until soldiers led all the doctors away and my family was sent to a school where hundreds of people whose families were missing had gathered. Everyone was loaded onto trucks and driven to the village, where I found them.

On the way back, I held my son in my arms. My friend helped carry the bundle of our clothes. We didn't have much left but this was no longer important as long as my family was together again.

That night, everything turned very noisy in our small camp. All our sadness and worries had disappeared. My son was just three years old. He had been sick very often and could not walk yet. My older son had died five months earlier. I sat looking at my child's face in the light of the campfire and felt very happy. If I had not met my son and wife, I would have been depressed all my life.

In the morning, I organized a makeshift camp for my family. We had no cooking pot but Than gave us one. Every day I went with Than to look for food. Sometimes we had to go into the forest to collect cassava, which we mixed with rice to stretch our supply. The soldiers had not distributed more rice. We were able to survive by helping and sharing the little that we had with each other.

Days and months passed. It began raining very hard. Our camps could not endure such heavy rain. The roofs of our shelters were made of tree leaves which only kept out the heat of the sun. Each time it rained, the water leaked through as if we were sitting in an open field. I had only a poncho to cover my wife and son and our clothes. Than and I would sit in the rain until it stopped. Life was very hard.

"We will not be able to live like this very long," I said to Than. "Our small children especially cannot endure this. The soldiers must have abandoned us here — we don't know when we'll get more rice again. We should go and stay in my home village on the eastern side of the Sangkhe River."

Than said we should leave soon while the soldiers were still fairly lenient, so we set off the next day. Along the way we passed a constant stream of people coming and going across the rice fields. We were fortunate not to have any trouble from the soldiers.

After resting along the way one night, we arrived at the river, where my friend and I split up because he found other relatives there. Than tried to get us to stay with him but I wanted to return to my own home village which was not far away. It would take only a few hours to get there. We parted not knowing if we would ever see each other again.

I learned that the people in my village had been moved about five kilometers to the east. We kept going and it was nearly 11 a.m. when we arrived. This new village had taken shape about one month before along a stream called O Mony. I met a lot of neighbors from my old village, who warmly welcomed me and prepared food for us. It was worlds different from the place we had come from. Here were plenty of food and supplies. That night, I slept peacefully.

The next morning, they took me to the cadre in charge of the village to request registration of my family. The cadre asked many questions and I told them the whole story. Finally, they agreed to let us stay.

In this village, they had already arranged to have people live in cooperatives and work groups. Every day, people went to work according to their orders. My family was allowed to solve the problem of shelter first. The chief of my team let me remove wood from a school to make a hut to live in. People went in groups to remove the wood from the school to build the collective. They even dismantled the monks' quarters and all the monks were moved out of the pagoda. Even if monks still lived in the pagoda they would not have any food because there were no villagers left to provide anything for them.

A week passed and I had built a small wooden hut for my family to stay in. Even though the floor was made of bamboo, and the roof and walls were made of old palm tree leaves, it was a good home.

The following day, I was assigned to transplant rice with other people. The work was not too hard for me because I had been born into a farmer's family.

Cooperative Number Five

It had been almost two years since the Khmer Rouge took power. The village on O Mony stream where I lived with my wife and children — we now had two — was called Cooperative Number Five. At first I did hard labor building houses, dams and irrigation canals. Later my job was to collect and saw firewood for the kitchen in my work group.

For a while the people in the village did not look so weak and beaten down when they came to get their rations from the kitchen. Some whispered and gossiped with each other and then gave a dry smile, seeming to have hope in something. When I came back every day from collecting firewood the cooks gave me an extra large ladleful of watery rice porridge to keep up my strength. The cook in the kitchen often told me, "If you find good firewood that does not produce much smoke, comrade, I will add some pure rice to your portion."

But then the atmosphere changed. The village became very quiet and empty. There had been 400 or 500 people living there, but suddenly it seemed abandoned. Where had everyone gone? Of course some had gone to the battlefield, some were in the hospital, others had disappeared secretly. Some had died of disease, starvation or dehydration. Their bodies became swollen and they could not walk so they lay under the sky waiting for death to come.

Step by step *Angkar* cut the food rations — from private eating to communal eating, from eating rice to eating porridge, from thick porridge to watery porridge. Finally they put only three tins of rice into a large pan to cook porridge for hundreds of people.

People died one after another. The duty to bury the bodies rested with me and another colleague named Leng. We were among the few able-bodied men remaining in the village — the others had gone to the front lines to work. Our job was to stay near the village and cut wood for the cooks.

When there was a body to bury, the chief of the team gave me an extra ladle of porridge. Nonetheless we lacked the strength to carry the bodies very far, nor dig the soil very deep. Out of my unit of 100 families, two or three people died each week. So many people died after a time that we were no longer shocked at having to bury them. I felt bad for the dead because we buried them without proper religious ceremonies and there were no monks to pray for them. We buried them like animals. Depending on what the family of the dead had, we might be able to make a rough wooden coffin out of spare planks. Otherwise we rolled them in a ricesack or a mat and buried them in unmarked graves not far from the village. It was my job to bury the ones who died of starvation or disease. We did not see the bodies of people who were executed. Those corpses were dumped in the forest away from the village.

One day — as far as I know it was December 28, 1977 — a large meeting was held at the cooperative. During the previous few days, teams of young militiamen had been going house by house, carrying machetes. They went from one end of the village to the other shouting that if anyone failed to go to the meeting, *Angkar* would drag them there.

On the day of the meeting, everyone seemed so shy and reserved — usually there was a lot of shouting and cheering before a meeting.

About 300 families with 1,500 to 2,000 people, including children and adults, lived in Cooperative Number Five. The year before there had hardly been any places to sit during the meeting because so many people were there. Since then, people had been disappearing secretly and steadily. Many seats were available at this year's meeting.

The main topic for the meeting was to choose the "spearhead forces" to launch a vigorous attack bringing in the rice harvest. Those who joined would get to eat cooked rice, not the watery porridge. When we heard the word *"rice"* our spirits soared although no one dared show it. There was only light applause at the announcement of rice, but everyone smiled secretly in their hearts.

Arrest

I was chosen to join the forces harvesting the rice and on December 29, 1977, I prepared to go. My wife packed a torn blanket and a plate and spoon in a rice sack for me. I was not too worried leaving my wife and children because the place where the rice was being harvested was only about two kilometers from our house. I knew I could sometimes come to see my family in the evenings.

Work in the rice field was not hard for me. I was assigned to carry rice bundles from the field to the threshing place. After two days there, while I was carrying my plate to get my ration of rice one evening, I glanced at the main road and saw an oxcart coming, a cloud of dust floating behind. When the oxcart got near, I recognized Comrade Luom, one of the commune chiefs. Without unyoking the oxen, he pointed at me and said I had been selected to cut rattan in the forest. Everyone turned to look at me. My heart plummeted because he chose only me out of a group of nearly 50 people.

"Comrade Nath, come with me," Luom said.

I replied quickly, "It's up to you, Brother — if you want me to go, I'll go."

Hardly had I spoken when he said sharply, "So let's go. Get your things and be quick."

"Let me eat first," I said.

"There's no shortage of rice where we're going," he said.

I didn't dare to argue with Luom so I went to get my bag from under a palm tree. He followed me and we got on the oxcart and headed out. When we got near my house, I jumped off.

"Where are you going?" he asked.

"I'm going to tell my wife — it will just take a minute," I said. As I told my wife about my new assignment, I had an ominous feeling. I didn't know how long I would be separated from my family. My wife and children watched me silently as I got on the oxcart and it lumbered down the road.

It was sunset when we arrived at the cooperative. They gave me a little rice with salt. As I ate, I wondered who would go with me to collect rattan and where we would go. Then Luom came and said we were going to Balat Pagoda, a cooperative about eight kilometers away, along the Sangkhe River. I collected my things and put them in the oxcart. We let the oxen drink and then yoked them and started off. I sat without talking until Luom startled me with his questions.

"Did you bring a machete and ax with you?" he asked.

"No, only a blanket and change of clothes," I replied.

"Oh! We need to get them from *Angkar*," he said.

As we drove along, the sky became darker and darker. It was 10 o'clock when we got to Balat Pagoda Cooperative.

"Nath, go sleep in the kitchen," Luom told me. "We will meet tomorrow morning."

Lying on an old mat on my back, I felt relaxed and fell asleep without knowing anything. It was still dark when a man's voice woke me.

"Nath ... Nath ... wake up. Get on the cart."

It was Luom, trying to wake me up. Half awake, I walked to the oxcart. Suddenly I saw the shadow of a large muscular man against the dark sky, holding a bundle of cow rope in his hands. He strode quickly toward me. I didn't know who he was. When he came near me he said, "Put your hands up!"

He grabbed my hands and forced them behind my back. I struggled and pushed him away. He moved back a few steps and then rushed at me again. This time I realized that it was Chhreung, known for being the savage butcher of Balat Pagoda Cooperative. I'd known Chhreung since he was young; he was from my village.

"What are you doing?" I asked him. I thought that maybe he was playing with me.

He didn't reply but kept pushing and trying to grab me. We struggled with each other but he was unable to tie me. Then Luom shouted,

"Let him tie you up!"

"What's happening to me?" I cried. "What have I done wrong?"

"I don't know," Luom said. "It's the order from the district chief."

I could hardly believe it. I stood like a statue. My body was a light as cotton. I allowed them to tie me like a pig.

Detention

They walked me into a wooden house where shackles and chains were waiting for me. Without uttering a word they put the shackles on my ankles and left.

The day that I'd imagined and feared had finally come. Thousands of questions were spinning in my head. I tried to think what I had done wrong. I was not thinking so much about my own life but how my wife and small children would survive without me.

It was past midnight when I heard the footsteps of Chhreung and several others coming, carrying a kerosene lamp. They handcuffed me behind my back, unlocked the shackles at my ankles, and ordered me to stand up. I was sure they were leading me away to kill me.

"Where are you taking me?" I asked Chhreung.

"To meet someone," he replied.

He walked me out of the wooden house and towards the shadow of a person waiting for me. When I had almost reached the man, I saw that it was Sien, the chief of the spying team in the cooperative. Chhreung handed me over to him.

"Friend, what is your name?" Sien asked. "What did you do wrong?"

"I don't know," I answered. "But they told me there was a letter from the district ordering my arrest."

"Let's go. There are others waiting for us on the main road," Sien said. He pushed my shoulder so I would walk. I begged them as we walked, "Don't tell my wife about this because she just delivered a baby a few months ago."

They didn't say a word. It was midnight and dead quiet. Walking in the dark, handcuffed, I had a terrible feeling of fear. They led me to the highway where an oxcart was waiting and I got in. I was surprised to find my cousin Serak, sitting on the cart, handcuffed like me. Serak was 19 and a senior in high school. When I saw him I didn't dare say anything. Phean got on the oxcart and said, "Let's go."

The oxcart driver urged the oxen on softly and the cart crawled in the blackening gloom. "I saw you were a very active worker," Phean said. "I don't know why the district ordered your arrest."

I didn't say anything. Phean asked about my family.

"I have two children," I told him. "The oldest is almost five years old. He is very thin and cannot work. The other is five months old."

As we went along, I realized we were on the way to Samraong Pagoda, where there was a district prison. When we arrived, two soldiers led us to the Pali school on the grounds of the pagoda. Inside I saw more than 10 prisoners, some sleeping, others sitting up with their feet shackled.

The soldiers shackled Serak and me at the ankles and released our handcuffs. Then they went out, locking the door. Scared and weary, I laid down and went to sleep.

When I woke up the sun was shining. Everything came back to me from the night before. I was still shackled. I looked around and saw that Serak had not woken up yet. On my right there were two others in shackles. I knew them very well; they were men from my cooperative. We just looked at each other without saying a word.

I heard the door being unlocked and two men came in carrying a bucket and a basket of plates. I woke up Serak. They put small rice bowls in front of the prisoners and served us watery porridge — one ladleful each with two or three grains of salt.

I looked at the porridge and felt so badly about my family. I wasn't hungry at all but I made an effort to lift the bowl to my mouth to swallow some of the gruel. Serak wouldn't eat at all even though I tried to persuade him. Then I lay down, resting my arm across my forehead, feeling no hope at all. I thought about the day that they would take me away to kill me.

The Three Satans

Deep in thought, I was startled by the sound of a motorcycle entering the grounds of the prison. Two soldiers, aged about 18 and 22, walked up and asked for Say Serak and Heng Nath, using the name I used to go by.

"That's me," I replied, my heart pounding.

"Unshackle him and walk him out," one of the soldiers ordered.

"You two must go resolve an issue with someone who has accused you of having breached a moral contact with them," the soldier said. That meant I was accused of violating the rules by having an illicit love affair with someone.

"Where are they?" I asked.

"You'll see them soon," the soldier answered.

They walked both of us out of the room and Serak and I got on the motorcycle with the two soldiers. One of them carried an AK-47 rifle.

"Where are you taking me?" I asked.

"To meet the woman who has accused you," he responded. I wondered what tricks they were using against me.

"I've never done anything morally wrong with any women," I told them.

"Okay. If the accuser says it was not you, you'll be free. Don't worry," he said.

I stayed still and looked around me as we drove. It was very quiet and there were no people in the villages we passed. They were taking me along the Sangkhe River, and we went through my old village. We drove through Battambang town on the eastern side of the river. The concrete houses and the market were all closed. It was very quiet, with no people walking around. Before April 17, 1975, the market bustled with activity every day.

At the iron bridge, the motorcycle turned south toward Kandal Pagoda, where we stopped. Two soldiers came up and tied our hands behind us with their *krahmas*. One of the soldiers walked me into the pagoda and another took Serak somewhere else. They led me to a room with five others and locked me in wooden stocks. I recognized one of the five as Vann Tep, the chief of the cooperative at Samdech Pagoda. He had been with the Khmer Rouge for many years before they defeated the government army. The cooperative was even nicknamed after him: Cooperative Ta Tep. I wondered why he was also shackled here. As far as I knew, he had acted like a king when he was in charge of the cooperative. Nobody had dared to look him in the his face. Now he was here in prison with me. This was revolution: it would always change like this.

The five men looked at me as if they wanted to know the newcomer. But the guard harshly ordered us to sleep, and forbade us to talk with each other. They gave us one bowl of rice gruel with a few grains of salt and six spoons. I didn't feel very hungry and stopped eating after two or three spoonfuls. One of the men sitting next to me asked quietly, "Why did you eat so little?"

I shook my head to indicate that I couldn't swallow the food, because my feelings and mind were elsewhere.

That evening around 7 o'clock, several men, one holding a name list and the other carrying an AK-47, came to take me out.

"Who is Heng Nath?" the oldest man asked.

"Yes, me," I answered, my heart plummeting and my body getting cold. Before they released my feet from the shackles, they handcuffed me behind my back and bound my shoulders.

They walked me into the forest behind the pagoda and I thought for sure I was going to be shot right there. But instead they pushed me into a small brick house, where they lit a lamp and told me to sit down. Hanging on the walls I saw long metal bolts, truncheons, plastic bags and whips. Under my chair were fresh blood stains.

As one of the men wrote, they asked me about my background: what I had done since I was ten years old, during the Sihanouk time, the Lon Nol time, and so on. I told them that I had been a student, then a painter — which was, after all, the truth.

"What was the problem that caused them to arrest you?" the interrogator asked. I said I didn't know.

"*Angkar* is not stupid," he said. "It never catches people who are not guilty. Now think again — what did you do wrong?"

"I don't know," I said again. "I was working in the base. *Angkar* assigned me to go off and find rattan and then they arrested me."

The interrogator told me to confess, or else he'd hurt me. I didn't have any answer. He tied the electric wire firmly around my handcuffs and connected the other end to my trousers with a safety pin. He sat down again.

"You've been reported to have been going around instigating people to oppose *Angkar*," he said. "Who is your network?"

"I don't know what you're talking about, Brother," I said. I didn't know what they thought I had done. At the cooperative I never had time to go around and see my friends, not a single one. It must have been a pretext to kill me. The man holding the gun laid it on the table and walked towards me. He connected the wire to the electric power and connected the other end to my bottom of my shorts.

"Now do you remember? Who collaborated with you to betray *Angkar*?" he asked.

I couldn't think of the words to answer them when he gave me an electric shock. My whole body went into a spasm and I passed out. When I came to I could hear a distant voice asking, "How many people in your network? Who are you communicating with?"

"No … brothers," I could only get those two words out before I fell unconscious again.

After they still couldn't get the confession they wanted out of me, they shocked me again so severely that I collapsed on the floor, my shirt completely drenched with sweat. When I woke up again, all I felt was a numbness in my ears and intense thirst. Eventually they lifted me up by the collar of my shirt.

I couldn't stand firmly because I had no energy at all. My lips and throat were completely dry. They shoved me out of the house, back to the room where I'd been that morning. The other prisoners looked at me with fearful eyes as the guards shackled me again. I said quietly to the other prisoners, "Let me drink some of that water."

They handed the water to me, causing me a moment of relief. But just as I was about to take a sip a strong hand knocked the container out of my hands. I looked up and saw the guard staring at me with horrifying eyes.

"Who allowed you to drink water!" he shouted. "What makes you so free? Sleep!"

I tried to plead with him again: "Brother, let me drink a little bit. My throat is so dry."

"No, you cannot," he said, pouring the water onto the ground.

I felt despair and lay on the floor to sleep. I was very anxious. How brutal they were! What was I guilty of that they tortured me so cruelly? If I was tortured the same way for two more days, I thought I surely would die.

When I woke up, I felt completely exhausted. I tried to sit up and looked around at the others shackled together with me. They were looking at me as if they wanted to ask me something. I looked down on my thigh and saw a large black burn mark where they had fastened the electric wire and pin the night before. One of my shacklemates asked me quietly, "How did they treat you last night?"

I shook my head and said, "They put me to electric shock. Look at my thigh. If they take me for interrogation again today, I don't know whether I can endure it or not." I stopped talking when I noticed that the guard was standing on the doorstep. He looked at me for a long time and then said, "What were you just whispering about? Speak up quickly."

My hands and legs turned cold and I answered with a trembling voice, "Yes, Brother, I was thirsty and was asking him for some water ..."

He didn't say anything. Actually I was not as thirsty as the night before, but it was a good excuse.

It was already noon. I was weak and fatigued but not very hungry. My biggest fear was that they would come and take me out again when it got dark. If they took me out to kill me I would be afraid only once. But now I was afraid all the time.

After eating each meal I would always stare at the door without blinking, afraid that those three men would come to call me out again. After a short while, darkness began to fall again. Just as I had feared, the three Satans in black uniforms appeared at the doorway. I was very frightened and sat up abruptly. A threatening voice shouted out, "Who is Phy Hieng? Get up!"

I was extremely glad, while also sorry for a new friend sitting near me. Phy Hieng's lips turned white and his hands and legs were shaking. He was handcuffed and tied with a rope and led away. I lay back down and let out my tension with a sigh. I was thinking of the torture that Phy Hieng was to get that night.

It was getting late, but Phy Hieng had not returned. I could hear threats and shouts from the interrogators once in a while. I tried to sleep but couldn't. What was happening to Hieng?

They had no mercy for other human beings. Their accusation of "*kmang*" — enemy — was so powerful. It separated fathers, mothers, children and siblings from each other. This word "*kmang*" made people from all levels feel so frightened.

I heard footsteps. I turned to see Phy Hieng walking in, his pale face completely drenched in blood. I felt panicked. His nose and ears were bleeding nonstop. They must have tortured him by putting a plastic bag over his head. That night I could not sleep at all because Phy Hieng moaned in pain all night long.

Transit to Tuol Sleng

Days and nights replaced each other and I'd been in Kandal prison almost a week. Only Phy Hieng and I had been taken out for interrogation during that time.

On the seventh morning, two guards came to our room with a list of prisoners in their hands. They called out the names Phy Hieng, Heng Nath, Van Tep and Top Tuom. It was January 7, 1978. Looking at the others, I started feeling panic again. They handcuffed the four of us and took us outside and made us sit down. Only then did I realize that the prison where we were detained had three stories. Before "Liberation Day," this place had been a Buddhist school, where monks came to study scriptures. But now it was a place to handcuff, shackle, torture and kill people.

An hour later, the guards came back and led us out toward two Chinese trucks with canvas covers. I had an ominous feeling because I'd heard in the cooperative about trucks carrying people to be killed at Bek Chan Airport every day. These trucks must be the ones they'd been talking about. Climbing up into the truck, I saw more than a dozen people sitting with their legs in shackles. I saw Serak, my cousin, among the prisoners. They inserted our legs into a shackle that was about 10 centimeters thick, and bolted it with a one-inch bolt, which they tightened with a wrench.

Around noon the truck drove off with 18 prisoners and three soldiers with AK-47 rifles to guard us. All of the prisoners looked completely desperate. Serak looked as if he wanted to say something to me but he didn't dare speak. He just stared at me and blinked his eyes. The truck left Kandal Pagoda and headed east. I looked through a small hole in the canvas and saw that we were heading toward Route 5. We must be going to Bek Chan Airport, I thought. But when we approached the airport the truck sped past. I was only a little relieved because then I thought they must be taking us to Kach Rotes, another large prison.

Half an hour, an hour, two hours passed by, but the truck kept up the same speed. I wondered where they were taking us. No answers. If they were taking us to kill us, why had they come so far? They wouldn't want to waste their gas. I was very exhausted and hungry. Along the bumpy road I was sitting awkwardly with my legs in the shackles. I couldn't move my body. I hadn't eaten or drunk anything the whole day.

It was getting dark and the truck continued on. Around 6 p.m. the truck slowed down and then stopped. One of the soldiers stood up and stretched.

"Hey you guys, stay still and don't talk. If you want to piss, here is a bucket. Piss in it," he said. He pointed at a bucket in the corner of the truck.

The soldiers got out. At first I didn't know why they stopped, but I realized they had stopped to eat dinner. Would they give the prisoners something to eat?

It was completely dark inside the truck. I could hear footsteps outside and then I heard them calling each other to eat. I swallowed my saliva from hunger. Maybe they would give us something to eat after they had eaten their dinner, I thought. We waited and waited. Finally the soldiers returned to the truck. One of them flashed an electric torch on the prisoners. Another took a wrench to secure the shackles, the bolts making an irritating creak. They tightened up the bolts until they were buried deep in the wood. Who would have hands strong enough to remove them?

"Be careful," the guard warned. "You are absolutely prohibited from touching the bolts."

They started up the engines. My truck went ahead. This time I didn't think of anything or wonder where they were taking me. I slumped over the shackle, trying to regain some energy. The road was so bumpy I could hardly bear it.

The truck went further and further. We could see each other's faces in the headlights of the truck behind us, coming through the gaps of the canvas which was blown up by the wind.

It was past midnight, but the truck still continued on. It stopped once in a while along the way. Each time the man who was sitting with the driver got down, probably to check in at the armed control points along the way. Then I saw dazzling light coming through the canvas: it must be Phnom Penh. I looked through the holes and saw electric lights and concrete buildings and houses, but everything was quiet. A little while later, the truck stopped. We had arrived at our destination. The tailgate was lowered and the truck was flooded with light. I saw beautiful villas and houses with lights in every one of them, and a large concrete building surrounded by fencing and barbed wire.

The cold January wind was blowing. I heard a telephone ringing from a large house. It was a sound I hadn't heard in three years. About 20 minutes later, two soldiers came, one with a bunch of handcuffs and the other with a flashlight. They ordered us to stick out our hands, and they cuffed me together with another prisoner named

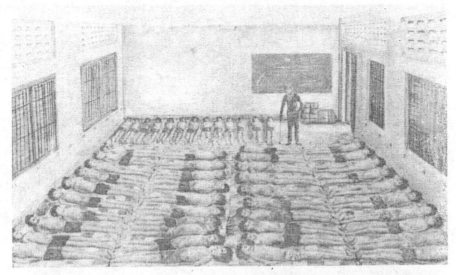

The S-21 secret prison of the Khmer Rouge, painted by Vann Nath

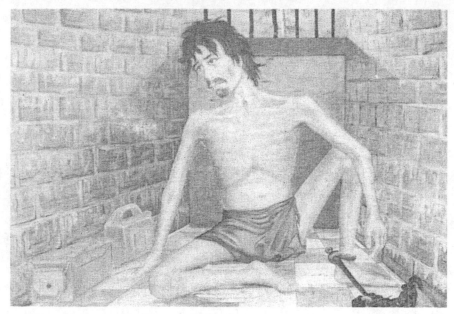

The S-21 secret prison of the Khmer Rouge, painted by Vann Nath

Vann Nath joined the PRK army after his release from Tuol Sleng.
Photo taken around 1980

Seven survivors of Tuol Sleng, 1980: Vann Nath is in the middle

The Khmer Rouge took photos of their victims before executing them. The photos are now on display in the Museum of Genocide
(Photo: Darren Whiteside)

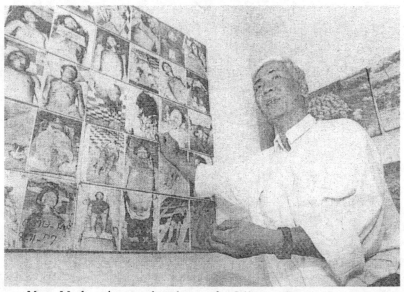

Vann Nath points to the photo of a fellow prisoner, a women who lept to her death rather than succumb to more torture
(Photo: Darren Whiteside)

The S-21 secret prison of the Khmer Rouge, painted by Vann Nath

The S-21 secret prison of the Khmer Rouge, painted by Vann Nath

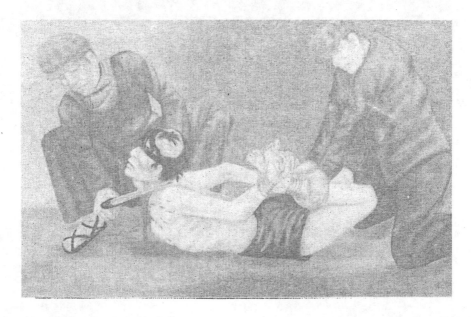

Vann Nath with one of the busts of Pol Pot made by the author.
Now on display in the Museum of Genocide, the bust was
defaced after 1977 (Photo: Darren Whiteside)

Vann Nath in front of one of the former classrooms used as a
cellblock in Tuol Sleng (Photo: Darren Whiteside)

After a hiatus of many years Vann Nath began painting
again in 1997, using the rooftop of his Phnom Penh home
as an open-air studio (Photo: David van der Veen)

Vann Nath today with his wife Kith Eng and children Simen (left),
17; Sineth (center), 14; and Narong, 7 (Photo: David van der Veen)

Chan Chath. They unshackled us and ordered us down. I lowered myself unsteadily, confused and not knowing where I was. They ordered us to squat in two rows in the dirt. On the left an 18-year-old boy sat at a small table with a book on it. He was holding a pen and staring at the prisoners. Then he shouted as if he had been angry with us for a long time.

"You, in front: What's your name? Where are you from? What district? What section? What region?"

"Yes, my name's Tob Tuom from district 41, section 4, northwestern region."

"Next!" he shouted in a threatening voice.

"My name's Heng Nath. During Sihanouk time, I was a school boy. Lon Nol regime, a painter. Revolutionary time, a farmer."

The answers were given one after another until everyone had done so. Then we were all blindfolded and ordered to stand up. They tied us all together by the neck and led us into S-21 prison.

"Walk, you guys!"

I was very frightened to hear their voices as well as the sounds of them beating someone at the back of the line. I was walking like a toddler because it was so dark, listening carefully to all the sounds around me. I didn't know how far I had come and suddenly I hit a sheet of corrugated iron in front of me, making a crashing noise. A shout burst out: "You, guy, walking like you have no eyes. You bastard!"

Feeling panicked I backed up quickly. But not before a heavy foot kicked me on the thigh, causing me to fall to the ground. But because of the handcuffs and the rope hooked around my neck I was able to get up quickly and walk ahead.

"Hey you guys, lift your feet when you walk! Ha ha ha ..."

I tried to raise my feet high for fear that I would stumble into something. They must be trying to make fun of us, I thought. They were so delighted to see people with no eyes, walking with their feet lifted up. I was frightened and wondered where they were taking me. Then I realized we were going into a building as we stepped up a few stairs. My feet touched a concrete floor and we were ordered to stop and sit down.

I bent to sit, feeling unsure of what place this was. What were they going to do? I heard the clock strike three in the morning.

"You, guy! What's your name? What did you do during the Sihanouk regime? The Lon Nol regime?" They'd already asked us these questions when we got off the trucks. Why were they asking us again? Every prisoner was interrogated again and then it was my turn. Afterwards, I felt someone undoing my blindfolds. At first my eyes were out of focus but then my vision cleared. In front of me was a chair with a camera set across from it.

"Go sit on that chair," the guard said, pointing at me.

The others handcuffed to me went with me but they sat on the floor as I was photographed. The guard took a picture of the front of my face, and then the side. Another guard measured my head and then they made an ID card. After me, they photographed the other people attached to me. Then they put our blindfolds back on.

First Night

"Stand up," the guard ordered. All the prisoners stood and they tied all of us together again by a rope around our necks. We walked in the dark. It was very difficult for me to stand and to walk — weak and blindfolded — so I concentrated on following the sounds of the footsteps of the person in front of me. They were leading us upstairs. There were many stairs to climb.

When we got to the top the guards ordered us to sit down. My legs were stiff and shaking. They removed the blindfolds. I was in a large room with a blackboard near the door. Near the blackboard were about 12 prisoners who were shackled. Some had short hair, some had long hair, some had their hair hacked off haphazardly as if the barber had been playing around. Their bodies were very thin and pale. I couldn't tell if they were men or women. The guards locked us 20 newcomers into iron leg shackles. We had to slip our ankles into metal rings which were attached to a long metal bar, with more than a dozen prisoners attached to one bar.

"If there is someone who knows how to read, read these regulations loudly for the others to hear," said the guard, a boy about 15 years old. After listening to the internal regulations, I sat down.

"Who let you do that!" the guard shouted. "Stand up! Get up! You're not free! You can't do what you want!"

"Take off your black clothes," he said. Unfortunately I was not wearing underwear. I said to the guards, "Brothers, I have no underwear."

"No problem," said the guard. "Take your clothes off."

I realized that this place was more strict than in Battambang. I knew that I could not persuade them not to make me take my clothes off, so I took them off. Twenty of the 32 prisoners were also naked.

A cool wind was coming in from the window and made me very cold. I sat with my arms around my knees trying to get warm. After a while, a guard brought in a pile of clothes and dropped them on the floor. I got a pair of yellow trousers and a long-sleeved shirt without buttons. I tried to figure out how I could put on the trousers since one of my legs was in the shackle. First I just put on the shirt but then I thought of a way. I inserted the trousers through the shackle of one leg, inching it through bit by bit until it had gone through. Then I inserted the other foot into the trousers. Afterwards I lay exhausted on the floor, without one grain of rice in my belly. I fell asleep without knowing anything.

I woke up early the next day, my body aching. I was famished and I wondered what kind of food they would give me when they let me eat. I wanted to sit up but I didn't dare because the regulations said that if we wanted to sit, we had to ask permission from the guards. I leaned closer to another guy from Battambang.

"We have no hope," I whispered. "Do you have a wife or children?"

"I have two small children," he said. "My marriage was arranged by *Angkar* 29 days before liberation. My wife and children are in difficulty right now without me. How about you? What happened to you?"

"Until right now, I don't know what happened," I replied.

"I think they arrested us without reason," he said. "If they doubt or suspect that in this three-year model regime, we've done something wrong, they do not trust us at all. Their revolutionary theory says, 'It's better to kill you by mistake than to keep you by mistake.' "

Then a man carrying porridge in a bucket on a shoulder pole came in the room. I was very excited because I realized food had come. Everyone got four small spoonfuls of porridge and some watery soup with banana leaves floating in it. It tasted delicious to me because I was so hungry.

But after a couple of spoonfuls, the food was all gone, and the guards ordered us to go to sleep. I lay down on the floor and realized that they were not going to give me water. I turned to a prisoner nearby, named Chath. His eyelids were drooping.

"Two or three spoons of rice — is that enough?" I asked. "I'm so hungry, if there was ten plates of rice it wouldn't be enough for me."

"Keep quiet, be careful," he said.

Restrained by the shackles, I tried to shift my aching body a little bit. As I lay there I thought about my life. What will happen to me in the future? Will I die soon? I thought about the prisoners who were there before me, and wondered how long they had been in that room. Eventually I fell asleep.

When I woke up, I wanted badly to sit up and drink some water. I had not had any water since the day before. I asked the guard if I could sit up and he said okay. I could see the coconut leaves moving in the wind outside the window. As far as I knew, it was already afternoon. I began to feel hungry and wanted to ask for some water but didn't dare.

Another prisoner called out, "Brother, I want to sit a little bit." The guard agreed. Then the same man asked for some water.

"Why do you ask me to drink water?" the guard yelled. He swore at the prisoner, calling him "*a-pret*," meaning the people who live in hell. I was glad I hadn't asked.

The sky began to darken. The electric power came on in the room and it was as bright as daylight. I lay back and looked at a small gecko on the ceiling that was catching insects around the electric light. The gecko was luckier than me, I thought, because it had plenty of insects to eat. My belly felt like it was almost touching my back bone. When will they give us another plate of rice porridge? Maybe they only gave one meal a day. If so we'd starve to death in less than half a month.

Then I heard the guards ordering us to wake up. I sat up quickly and saw that the rice porridge had come. I swallowed my spit because I was so hungry. They were passing the plates out, the same as the morning. I wanted to save some but I was too hungry. The others were the same and in a blink of an eye, everything was gone and the bowls were licked clean.

This was my second night there. I couldn't sleep because the guards were constantly coming in to check the shackles because they were afraid we would escape. My God, the piece of iron was as big as our thumbs. How could our feet get free?

Then we heard a voice order, "You all get up." After sitting up, I saw a small boy, about 13 years old, standing with a meter-long rod made of twisted electric wire.

"Why are you still sleeping? It's nearly dawn," the boy said. "Don't be lazy. Do some exercises."

"How can I exercise, Brother?" a prisoner asked.

"How stupid you are, old coot," the boy said. "Get the shit buckets and put them under the shackle bars and jump together."

All the prisoners followed his instructions. The noise of shackles and buckets clanged throughout the room. I tried to jump up a few times together with other prisoners. But how could we do that with one ankle fastened up to the shackles and the other foot jumping? And we had no energy at all.

After about two minutes the noise of the shackles turned silent. I looked around and saw some people standing, while others were sitting down.

"Who told you to sit down!" the guard shouted. "Wait until I tell you to do so."

Because I was afraid of his electric wire rod, I tried to jump again. If we didn't follow orders, he would beat us. A while later he told us to stop.

"O.K., stop! Are you feeling good?"

"Yes, good," we answered in unison.

"All right! You can sleep again now," he said.

First Month

After living that kind of life for several days my body began to deteriorate. My ribs were poking out and my body was like an old man of 70. My hair was overgrown like bamboo roots, and had become a nest for lice. I had scabies all over my body. My mind and spirit had flown away. I only knew one thing clearly: Hunger.

Every four days, they gave us a bath. They brought hoses up from downstairs and sprayed everyone from the doorway. If you were on the far side of the room, like I was, you didn't get very wet.

Each day they would take some prisoners out of my room to be interrogated. They would handcuff and blindfold the prisoners before they left the room. Sometimes some of the prisoners came back with wounds or blood on their bodies, while others disappeared. Prisoners who had been there when I arrived started dying in the room, one by one. If a prisoner died in the morning, they would not take him out until night.

I lived that way for more than 30 days. I was never released from the shackles, and had to ask permission every time I sat up. If I needed to defecate I asked the guards to bring the bucket over.

One day I felt unusually weak and exhausted. I could not hear anything clearly — it felt like my ears were filled with cotton. More prisoners were brought in that day, bringing the total number of people in the room to about 50, and they put in another long iron bar across the room for the new inmates' shackles. I whispered to Chath, the man next to me, "Brother, I don't think I can make it another ten days. I'm so hungry and I can hardly hear or see."

"I'm the same — we have no hope now," Chath said, his eyes swimming in tears. "We will surely meet the same fate as those who were here before us."

"Brother, how long have we been here?" I asked.

"About one month now," he replied.

I grew quiet, and looked out the window at the leaves and fruits of the coconut tree outside. I wanted to eat those coconuts very much. Each night if any crickets or grasshoppers fell down from the electric lights above, we would scramble for them and toss them into our mouths as if they were delicious. When the guard caught us, he would smack our heads as hard as he could with his thick sandal made of rubber auto tire, giving us black eyes or bloody noses.

This particular morning, after eating my plate of rice porridge, I dozed like the other prisoners. Then I heard someone calling my name in the next room. Not long after, three men came and stood at the window of my room.

"Is there someone named Nath in this room?" one of the men shouted.

My hands and feet turned cold, realizing that it was my turn now. All the other prisoners turned to stare at me except for Brother Chath. He seized my hands firmly and looked into my face as if he wanted to tell me something. I tried to control my heart so that my tears wouldn't flow.

"I'd like to say good-bye for now," I told him. "If I don't come back today, we won't see each other again."

Chath could not manage to say anything to me. He let my hands go.

Meeting Deuch

The room became noisy and active. In order to take me out, the guards had to free more than 20 other prisoners who were shackled to the same iron bar: I was at the end of the bar. The guards handcuffed all the prisoners together before they removed the ankle rings one by one. Then they tied my hands behind my back with hammock rope.

I was so weak I could barely stand up. I took a step and the guards held both of my forearms like a child who was just learning to walk. I couldn't feel anything at all because I was 80 percent dead. As I left the room, I looked outside and dimly realized that I had been on the third floor.

"Go down carefully or you'll fall face down," the guards told me.

I made my way down the stairs with my legs shaking, propped up by the guards. As we walked the guards asked, "How long have you been able to paint pictures?"

I was surprised by this question and thought it was some sort of trick. "Since 1965," I replied.

"Can you draw beautiful pictures?" they asked.

"Not really," I said.

Along the way I stole some glances around. All the prison guards were watching me as I passed. They led me to a building where I saw a man sitting on a sofa. He was thin, about 40 years old. Later I learned his name was Deuch and that he was the chief of the prison.

"Let him sit down," he told the guards.

I was so frightened that I sat cross-legged on the floor.

"No, don't sit that way," the man said. "I don't like it. Stretch your legs. Unfasten his legs — but don't run." I stretched out my legs and the guards untied my hands. My hands were numb and could hardly move because they'd been tied so tightly. Looking around, I realized I was not in an interrogation room

The two guards seemed to treat the man on the sofa with a lot of respect. It was clear that he was not a low-ranking man. His words seemed so powerful and his bodyguards appeared like mice cowering in front of a cat.

Deuch asked me how many years I had been a painter, and I could tell he had read my biography. They brought out a large photograph of Pol Pot and put it in front of me.

"Do you know this person?" Deuch asked.

"No, I don't," I said.

"Try and make a guess. Say who it is."

"No, I don't dare, because I don't know him."

"Don't be afraid. We're telling you to make a guess."

"Well, it's … Brother … Brother … Khieu Samphan," I ventured.

They burst out laughing.

"No it's not, it's not Brother Hem," Deuch said, referring to Khieu Samphan by his revolutionary name, Hem. "Do you know why you've been moved down here?"

I said I didn't know.

"Well listen carefully. I want a realistic, clear, correct and noble reproduction of this photograph. Can you do that?"

I replied that I could not guarantee anything because I hadn't painted for two or three years. I would try to do my best, I told them, but right then I couldn't even stand up.

"Okay, it's no problem," Deuch said. "We'll give you three days off — but not to sleep. You must check the other painters' pictures to see if there is anything wrong. Do you get it?"

I felt very relieved because it seemed they weren't going to kill me now. They'd assigned me a specialized job. I would have to try hard. That would be difficult because I had no energy at all and could hardly hold a spoon much less a paint brush. While my thoughts were drifting further and further, Deuch said:

"There is something else you must know. I have a hint for you. Staying here, you must know how to put yourself lower than the masses. The important thing is to be gently humble. Can you do that?"

"Yes, I can do that," I replied.

"There is a person in charge of this workroom. If you want to do anything, you must ask his permission," he said, pointing at a man standing near the wall. "Meng, you have a colleague now," he said.

Three Days Off

Deuch had them take me outside to cut my hair and fingernails and let me take a shower. It was February 2nd or 3rd, around 10 in the morning. I could see the sky and it was the first time I'd felt the sun on my skin in a long time. The feeling of warmth was so strange.

After my shower they gave me clean black clothes to wear. I had no idea what was going to happen. I'd stopped thinking about anything. Maybe they were going to kill me, maybe not. It didn't matter. Wisdom and spirit had flown away from me. All I thought about was my stomach. If they gave me food, that was enough. Food was the priority.

They gave me a big plate of rice to eat, the first solid food I'd had in many weeks. At first I couldn't eat it because my mouth didn't work. I stuffed the rice into my mouth but it was hard to chew and an almost unbearable pain shot through my jaw. Then the guards told me that I had to eat slowly otherwise I could die from overeating.

I was not the first person they had let out of that room. There were three others who'd gotten out already. Two were painters, one a stone sculptor. During the three days I was allowed to rest, the guards had me sit with the three others to watch them work. The first day, when the guards left in the evening to eat, I walked over to the other two workmen.

"Have you been down here for a long time?" I asked them quietly.

One of the workers turned to me and smiled. "Almost one year," he said.

"Brother, if I do anything wrong, please let me know. I'd like to thank you in advance."

The other workman, named Pol Tuoch — his nickname was the Sculptor because of his skill in that work — had pus-filled scabs on his arms and legs. I walked over to him, but he didn't look up from the sculpture he was working on. After several minutes, he drew a deep breath and turned to me.

"Just let things be," he said. "Death stays close to us. You must not be careless."

I remained silent and asked him nothing more. I walked back and sat down on the floor, thinking. When I was shackled day and night, I had come to grips with the fact that I was going to die soon. So why should I worry now when I was much more relaxed, with my hands and legs free, and had food and clothes? If I was to die, let it be so. But one thing tugged at my heart: Had my wife and children also been arrested and brought here to be abused and killed? Why should they suffer because of my false arrest? Was it somehow my fault?

I wondered who the man in the photograph was, the man whose portrait Deuch wanted me to paint. When I was in the countryside, we thought there was no one with a higher rank than Khieu Samphan, the Khmer Rouge chief of state. Why had another man appeared? Was he higher than Khieu Samphan?

It was getting late in the evening, but the guards still hadn't brought us dinner. I could only think about food, but didn't dare to ask. I still felt unwell. How many more days would it be before I regained my energy, I wondered. Don't think too much about the future, just think of what is in front of you, I told myself.

The rice wagon arrived and the guard ordered us to go eat. We walked in a group out of the room. I was very glad because this is what I'd been dreaming about and waiting for. Oh God, you must have given me so much mercy on this day. I felt like I couldn't get enough to eat. When I stopped it was as if I hadn't eaten anything. But the others had stopped, so I had to stop as well. As I washed the bowls, I looked at the rice stored under the stairs. I thought of my shackled friends upstairs and how happy they would be to get some rice — even just a spoonful.

After eating, the other artists had gone back to the workroom. I didn't dare hang around any longer and followed them upstairs. I sat watching them work as I had in the morning. Darkness prevailed over Tuol Sleng. It was about eight o'clock. The guard tuned into the national radio station, which was full of news about the nation's rice production in accordance with *Angkar's* goals: the most glorious, the most wonderful. At the same time I could hear screams of pain from every corner of the prison. I felt a twinge of pain in my body at each scream. Even at this time of night they were still interrogating the prisoners. When I was detained upstairs I could also hear this but not as loud. I could hear the guards demanding the truth, the acts of betrayal, the names of collaborators. I had undergone this in Battambang, but never here. When would they take me for interrogation again, I wondered. Oh God, please help me avoid such an interrogation! I could not endure it. I wondered where I would sleep that night. I heard four or five men coming, and the room guard jumped up. I rushed to stand, to show my respect. The men walked in and said my name, as if they had known me for a long time.

"Have you eaten enough?" they asked.

"Yes, enough, sir," I said, lowering my head.

"If you've had enough, let's talk about work. After resting for three days, you must paint one piece to show you can paint like the others do. Can you do that?"

"Yes, but I cannot guarantee that it will be as good as the others' because I haven't painted in a long time," I said.

"That's all right. The important thing is to make an effort. If you try, you will be successful."

I knew nothing was more important than trying. This is what I had to do in exchange for keeping my life. After chatting for a while, they went out. It was already 11 o'clock at night. I wondered when they would let us go to sleep. The wind was blowing outside, leaving me chilled and shivering. The screams had stopped and the prison was quiet. I glanced through the window and saw a man in black uniform coming. It was the same man who had escorted me to the workroom that morning,

"Hey, go to sleep," he said, as he walked me outside. "You must try really hard. This is the opportunity for you to show your faithfulness and make the Party trust you. Remove the unnecessary feeling. Sharpen your thoughts and focus on the core duty that the Party has entrusted you to do. Do you hear me?"

"Yes, Brother."

He did not take me to the old place to sleep in shackles again. Instead we walked to another building opposite Building E and went upstairs. I stole a glance through the window and saw emaciated prisoners detained in various cells. I didn't dare look at them for long in case the guard saw me. He took me up to a room on the second floor and locked me in. A teenage guard stood outside the door. Inside there were eight other workmen sleeping on mats with blankets covering them. As I went to lay down, I realized that none of the people there were shackled. This was the first night my legs were free. I smiled in my heart and touched my ankles which had been shackled for more than a month. The wounds still hurt. I lay on a mat next to an older man, who was still awake. He looked at me with wondering eyes.

"Where are you from, nephew?" he whispered.

"I come from Battambang. I have been detained upstairs for over one month before they took me down this morning. And you, Uncle?" I asked.

"One year now," he said, sighing deeply.

I was shocked. A year is so long, especially to go without seeing family. He told me he was from Phnom Penh, and had been working at Chakangre Power Plant when he was arrested. We heard footsteps at the window and stopped talking.

When I got up in the morning, I saw the other workmen looking at me quietly. I smiled at them to express greetings. They smiled back at me. I was very pleased. After folding up my blanket I sat up like the others. The door opened and the guard ordered the carpenters to leave, leaving me alone. I wondered where the three other artists had slept. A little later the door opened again. "Painter, come out," the guard said. He walked me downstairs to the painting room.

"Did you sleep well last night?" the guard asked.

"Yes, I did, Brother," I said, calling him "Brother" to be polite even though he was only about 16 years old. When I arrived at the workroom, the three other artists were already working. This day I had regained some energy. To avoid sitting around with nothing to do, I made a proposal to the room guard.

"Brother, I want to make a frame for the picture I will begin painting in three days," I said. The guard agreed, and came back later with a carpenter.

"In my opinion it would be better if the painter can come to my workroom later for a minute so he can make sure I am making the frame correctly," the carpenter said. He winked at me as if he had a secret to tell. I turned to the guard to see if he agreed. The guard looked as if he suspected nothing, but I was afraid to ask permission to leave. The carpenter understood the situation, and standing up to go, repeated the request.

"Hey you, Tuon! Why are you saying the same thing again! I'll let him go," the guard said, using derogatory and abusive language with Tuon, who was old enough to be his grandfather. I was scared and didn't dare look at the guard's face, but Tuon's face showed no expression as he walked out. Was it a normal everyday thing for him to be insulted this way, I wondered. He didn't seem to pay it any mind. I knew the guard was ignorant and did not know the difference between right and wrong. He had been poisoned by the Khmer Rouge to hate and kill human beings without regret. He had no tolerance and no sentimental feelings, and thus was a strong force for the Party.

After lunch, the room guard took me to the carpenter's workroom. I didn't dare look around as I followed him along a thick fence made of barbed wire. He led me to a long wooden shed with a corrugated metal roof. The shed was divided into sections for carpentry, cages for pigs, and a kitchen. In the carpentry section, I saw Tuon cutting wood with an electric saw. Because of the noise from the machinery and his absorption in his work, Tuon didn't realize we were standing nearby. Then he spotted us and switched off the saw so we could hear each other. He showed me how he was going to make the frame. When the guard stepped off to look at the pigs, Tuon spoke to me in a low voice.

"It's not that I don't know how to make the frame," he said. "I wanted you to come for a chat." While continuing to work, he said he had been the head chief monk in a pagoda but had been disrobed by the Khmer Rouge in 1975 and taken to this prison. He had been here two years now. In the carpenter's hall, there were about 10 workmen who were all prisoners. They all looked at me out of the corners of their eyes because I was a newcomer. I wanted to talk to them very much, but time didn't allow me to. The guard came to take me back to the painting room.

First Painting

Three days later, I had enough energy to stand up for short periods of time and the ringing in my ears had gone. I started my first painting: a large portrait of Pol Pot, three meters by one-and-a-half meters. They had me paint in black and white, based on the black-and-white photograph. I told them I had not specialized in black-and-white painting, but they told me to experiment. My first day at work I was very nervous but tried not to show it outwardly. The guards were watching me through the window. I held my spirit and tried not to be afraid as I stood looking at the picture I had carefully copied from a photograph. A bit later, I had control over the main points of the picture. I used lamp soot to lightly shade it. From morning till night, I didn't dare to leave the picture except for meals. It was already 11 o'clock, but I went to sleep without having finished half of the work. I couldn't sleep that night because I was afraid they would say I didn't do the work well. But finally I decided to leave my life with my destiny and God.

The next morning, I got right to work on the picture again. I looked out the window and saw some prisoners pulling one another on a long chain of handcuffs. They were all blindfolded. They had thin bodies like corpses. Some were naked, while others had only shorts but no shirts. I didn't dare look for long because I was afraid of the guard sitting in the room. But before I could turn my face back he shouted: "Hey! What are you looking at! Do your work!"

Then he went out, closing all the windows and locking the door behind him. Noting the quiet moment, I walked close to the sculptor.

"Brother, where are they taking the prisoners this morning?" I asked him. "Some were kicked when they could not walk."

The sculptor didn't reply and looked at me as if he were bored with my question. Still doubtful, I walked to the windows and looked through the small gaps again. Oh God! Those prisoners were all from my room. I remembered one of them most clearly — Chath. Where were they taking the prisoners? Were they taking them back to the cooperatives to work on the farms? Or were they leading them off to their deaths? If so, it was beyond brutal to kill such a group of people. If they had not taken me down to work on paintings of Pol Pot, I would have been among them. There were no answers.

The engines started up as several trucks moved off. As the noise receded, I turned back to my picture with my heart filled with what had just happened. I didn't have any motivation to paint. I picked up the photograph of Pol Pot for a close look at it. Surely this photograph must be of the supreme leader of this regime, I thought. His face looked smooth and calm, but I knew he must be savage and very evil. I wondered how he could look so pleasant yet treat people so cruelly, torturing and killing people of the same Khmer blood without feeling any regret. Or was he a Khmer person? With such an appearance and complexion, he could be Chinese.

In the nine days since I'd come downstairs to paint, I noticed that the prison was very active and busy. Prisoners were being trucked in day and night — sometimes until two o'clock in the morning. Oh, the Khmers, both myself and others, why were we such a miserable people? What were we guilty of? I could not think of what I had done wrong. When I was upstairs, I would hear them swearing at the prisoners: "You are CIA!" or "You are KGB!"

The words "CIA" and "KGB" were the main cause of death for people. In fact, none of us knew what the CIA and KGB were. I just knew that CIA were the secret agents from the United States and KGB were the agents from the Soviet Union. But, beyond that I knew and understood nothing.

During the previous regimes, I only cared about my career so far as it earned me a living. I wasn't concerned about politics or the struggles for power. I didn't care who would take over or who would lose power. But now they put citizens from the very low classes in charge, as if they were very high politicians.

If we looked at the range of their leadership, we saw that almost 70 percent of them came from the farming class. They were shouting that they hated the high officials because the high officials would tread upon the inferiors and the weak. But now, when they came to power, they not only treaded upon the people but killed millions of their countrymen. This was what they called "the blazing revolution with greatest leap, most glorious and most wonderful."

They would not be satisfied until they could turn the entire country as quiet as a forest for burying the dead. During my life I had already come through three regimes: the Sangkum Reastr Niyum of Sihanouk, the Khmer Republic of Lon Nol, and now the Khmer Rouge's "Democratic Kampuchea." How many more regimes would I have to live through? Oh, Khmers! Our race would surely disappear if we had two or three more regimes of this type.

Peng's Threat

Days and nights went by without stopping and my health — both physical and spiritual — got better. I'd now been downstairs for more than two weeks.

Deuch, the prison chief, came in three or four times a day to comment on my paintings, and a guard watched us all the time. Every day I worked from 6 in the morning until lunch, and then on until midnight. Three times a day I saw prisoners being led to the interrogation areas. They were questioned from 7 to 11 in the morning, and in the afternoon from 2 to 5 and again in the evening from 7 to 11. They would take them outside of Tuol Sleng to the houses surrounding the prison, which were interrogation places.

After I tried for five days, the picture I painted did not come out exactly like the photograph. I was worried that they would not be very happy with it. When the painting was almost done, Deuch came by to inspect it. My heart was thumping.

"Does it look like the photograph?" he asked each time he came in.

"No, not yet," I replied. I didn't dare to say whether it looked right, preferring to leave it to him to decide.

His bodyguard Peng spoke up: "It don't look right to me."

Deuch said, "Though it doesn't look just like the photograph, I'm satisfied that Nath has tried very hard."

I then asked if I could paint in natural colors. Deuch agreed and assigned Peng to find watercolors.

Peng was a brutal guard, the most feared of all. His daily work was to kill people as ordered by his leaders. I never dared to look Peng in the face. I was more afraid of him than a young sheep is afraid of a tiger. Anytime my eyes met his I felt shaky. It was he who ordered and shouted at the prisoners who were taken out every day. After his boss left, Peng waited behind to speak to me.

"Hey guy, tell me what materials you need," he said. "But if you get these things and cannot do the job right, don't worry — my hands will welcome you." I knew he meant he would torture me. At first I did not feel intimidated because I was sure I could paint better in color. After Peng left, my friends looked at me, worried about my fate if I could not paint the picture properly.

That night, the room guard took me up to sleep at midnight as usual. As I lay on my mat in my usual place next to the carpenter, I thought about the Peng's threats. What was his role in this prison? The carpenter was still awake, lying with one of his hands on his forehead, smoking a cigarette. I covered my face with a scarf to avoid being seen by the guards outside and whispered quietly to him:

"Uncle! Do you know the guy named Peng? What does he do in this prison?"

I peered through the scarf and saw him looking at me anxiously. "Why do you ask?" he asked in a low voice.

"Because I never met him before, Uncle," I replied.

"Peng is the chief butcher who is brutal beyond words," he said. "His core duty is to kill people. Any time he comes around, nobody dares look at his face. He hits Tuon's head with his knuckles every day. There is another guy named Huy, who is also a chief butcher.

You must be careful, Nephew. You must make sure that you work hard enough so that Deuch is not angry with you. As far as I know, they have taken many artists down from upstairs, but they usually disappear after not more than ten days. You must be a bit careful."

The carpenter's warning made me feel light as cotton. Of course, it was Peng I saw the other day, holding the rod and ordering the prisoners out, including my friend Chath. My destiny was hanging on this last picture I was painting!

The carpenter continued in a low voice: "The other day, he gave me two long machetes to sharpen from morning till night. When I told him that they were already sharp enough, he ordered me to continue sharpening them. I don't know what he used them for. But as far as I can tell, they are for nothing other than killing the prisoners."

"Where do they take the prisoners to kill, Uncle?" I asked.

"How could I know, when we are all prisoners here? All right now, go to sleep and get some energy for tomorrow." He soon fell asleep, snoring loudly, leaving me alone with my thoughts until I too fell asleep.

In the morning, I went and reworked the black-and-white painting again. After lunch, I saw Peng standing at the window of my room.

"Here, guy, here are your materials," he said. Two young soldiers emptied a bag of art supplies in the middle of the room. I could see they were quality materials, including brushes and color paint.

"Have you got everything?" Peng said.

I told him it was sufficient.

"Okay then, keep your word. If you cannot do the work, just wait and see," he said as he walked off. I turned to my friends in the room, intending to ask their opinions. But it seemed no one had any ideas.

I started to paint in color, and three days later produced a beautiful color painting. I had tried my best, knowing my fate was tied to the picture. Through the window a group of guards had gathered to look at the painting, although Deuch had not yet come. I sat in front of the painting anxiously, checking and rechecking and asking my colleagues in the room for comments. The other artists and sculptors gave me some feedback on how to make the picture even better.

After dinner, my friends and I went back to work as usual. It was a bit late in the evening, but Deuch still had not come. I was very anxious, wanting the affair settled once and for all to rid me of the overwhelming doubts in my mind. I knew clearly that this was my last chance. There wouldn't be a second one because Peng, the chief butcher, had already said so.

A while later I heard footsteps and saw Deuch enter, accompanied by Peng and another man. Standing next to the wall, I waited for their reaction, feeling shaky and chaotic.

Deuch stood silently in front of the painting for several minutes and then burst into a loud laugh. "Good ... Good," he said. "It's all right."

These few words meant the difference between life and death for me.

"Meng, what do you think?" Deuch asked one of the other artists.

"Yes, it's quite nice, although it doesn't look exactly like the photograph yet," Meng responded.

"Er ... I know, but I want to ask if you yourself could paint like this," the chief said.

"I can," said Meng, "but it would take a long time." Meng was an unusually short man, but he used big words, and was full of pride. I felt very afraid whenever he talked to the prison chief because it seemed he did not humble himself enough.

"Nath, listen!" Deuch said, turning to me. "This painting is not completely right yet, but if there is any improvement in the next painting you will get a reward."

The three men walked out, leaving me some hope. As long as they were happy, I knew I would survive. That night I felt very relieved. Lying on my mat I turned to the old carpenter. Before I could say anything, he asked if I had finished the painting and whether it was all right. I told him there were still some problems with the painting, but Deuch seemed content with it for now.

"Okay, work hard," the carpenter said. "As long as they are satisfied, you will be able to live for a bit longer."

The carpenter and I stopped talking. It was quite cold outside and we could hear the interrogators' shouts and threats and the prisoners' screams of pain. These were sounds I heard all the time.

A Friend Disappears

Days and months passed by, and I finished another painting. This one was much better than the first, and Deuch was now very cordial with me. The reward they'd promised was to give me five packs of cigarettes. The prison guards were now very friendly with me and some young guards secretly came to see me during the night. They asked me to paint some colorful pictures of villagers, people planting rice, and people harvesting. When I had free time I painted pictures for them with approval from the room guard.

One day, after painting until about 11 in the evening, I was getting ready to go up to my room to sleep. I saw Peng, the chief butcher, looking through the window, sending a shiver through my spine. He had been gazing at me a long time.

"Meng, come here," he called out to my colleague. "Put on your shirt and come out."

Meng grabbed his shirt, turned to me with a smile, and walked out. The room guard then took me up to my room to sleep as usual. In the morning when I went back down to work, I didn't see Meng. I didn't ask the others because the room guard was standing nearby, but waited until he went to lunch.

"Brother, where did Meng go? Why hasn't he come to work?" I asked.

"How would I know, we all are the same," the sculptor replied.

"Maybe he's been set free and gone back to the cooperative?" I asked.

"I don't know," said Khun. "But as far as I know, none of the prisoners here have ever been freed. Maybe he's been sent to paint signs outside."

When we sat down to eat later there were only three of us. I was not sure what to think. If Meng had been sent out to work, he would be back by now. He'd been missing since the previous night. Maybe he'd really been sent back to the cooperative to work.

One day, two days, and then a week passed and we had heard nothing about Meng. I was sure he must have gone back home and didn't think about him anymore. One night I was almost asleep when I heard someone calling me loudly from downstairs.

"Comrade, tell the painter to come down here!"

I was startled as the door flew open. "Painter, go downstairs," a guard said. Trying to collect my thoughts, I realized it must be around midnight. Why were they calling us back to work? I felt afraid and my heart began to thump erratically. Downstairs I felt even more anxious when I saw Tuoch and Khun working as if it were normal, although they gave me a mysterious look.

"Get on with your work, Nath," the room guard shouted.

I quickly grabbed the photograph and began preparing the paint. About 15 minutes later, I heard the noise of chains being dragged across the floor toward me, mixed with the sound of a man shouting threats.

"Walk faster, damn you!"

Glancing at the window I saw a man chained from his neck to his ankles, with bandages covering bloody wounds all over his emaciated body. I almost fell backwards. I recognized him very well: it was Meng.

What was he guilty of that he had been tortured like this? I'd been dreaming about him seeing his family for many days. But no, he had been suffering.

One of the prison guards dragged Meng to the middle of the room. Then Deuch and his bodyguards appeared. I didn't dare look at Meng anymore and turned to focus on my painting. I tried to look at the picture without moving my body.

"Hey Meng, what have you promised us? Follow your words!" Deuch threatened. "Nath, look over here. Look at this bad guy."

I quickly turned towards Meng, who was looking at me as if he were asking for my help. I got off my chair and sat on the floor. I turned to Tuoch and Khun, who remained quiet, their faces pale from fear. At the same time, Meng crawled on his hands and knees towards me, dragging his chains behind. He looked up at me, his face dripping with tears.

"Nath, why are you looking so nervous?" Peng shouted at me.

There were about ten people in the room. Prison guards were silently crowding at the window to see inside. I was sitting, and Meng was crawling towards me. He saluted me three times slowly with the palms of his hands together.

"Sorry," he said.

No sooner did Meng speak, Deuch kicked him in the head. Meng fell to the floor.

"Damn you, you have not given up your bad ways," the guard shouted. "You are afraid of being base just for using the word 'I'."

Poor Meng was sitting with difficulty, the heavy chains hanging on his body. It tore my heart to see such a brutal thing happening in front of me. I turned to the other workmen sitting nearby. They were looking down at the floor. The atmosphere was unbearable.

"I am sorry, Brother!" Meng said in a shaky voice. Then he apologized to Tuoch and Khun.

"Take him out," Deuch ordered. "I can't stand to see his face anymore."

Meng was pulled out of the room, his chains dragging after him.

"Now you guys. What do you think about Meng?" Deuch asked us. "In my opinion he is no use anymore, because he is so tricky and arrogant. He is a snob, not knowing who the superiors are and who the subordinates are. I've seen him telling Nath things to do every day, while Nath's just allowed himself to be used quietly. It's better to use him to make fertilizer, don't you think?"

Deuch laughed cruelly and asked, "Is that right?"

No one answered. I looked out of the corners of my eyes, hoping the other two workmen would answer. But they were looking at the floor. I felt very stressed, almost out of breath. Nobody dared give their ideas. But Deuch insisted on asking again.

Unable to bear the tension, I decided to break the poisonous atmosphere and take a risk to help save a friend.

"Excuse me, Brother. I would like to ask you to tolerate Meng this once. He is really a bit snobby, but he will surely change since he's been punished. Please, Brother, pardon him this once. If he then does not realize his mistake, you can make your own decision."

Deuch laughed harshly. "Nath dares vouch for Meng! And how about Khun and Tuoch?" he said turning to the two, who both nodded their heads and quickly agreed.

"Okay," Deuch said. "But there must be three conditions, Nath. First Meng is not allowed to smoke. Secondly, he is only allow to walk within five squares of the floor from his painting. Third, his ankles must be chained. And Nath must be responsible for all of these conditions. If you fail to follow them, then you must get the punishment instead of Meng, all right?"

I agreed and Deuch walked out of the room with his bodyguards. It was already one o'clock in the morning and I went upstairs to sleep, overcome by waves of fear and panic.

The next morning, my heart was still full of the terrible events of the previous night, but I was relieved to have been able to save a friend's life. Though Meng was a bit mischievous, he did not deserve death. I had no idea why Deuch agreed with my suggestion. Maybe they wanted to spare Meng in order to keep using him.

The prison guards brought Meng into the workroom the next three days. They treated him less roughly, only chaining his ankles and leaving his hands free. When he arrived the first morning he walked straight to me, raising his hands to salute me.

"Thank you very much, Brother, for saving my life," he said. Then he walked over to Tuoch and Khun and thanked them also. I felt more relaxed to see Meng looking fresher than the other day. Not long afterwards, Deuch came in.

"Hey Meng, have you thanked these people for saving your life? But don't forget, you only get once chance."

"Yes, Brother," Meng replied, bowing his head.

After that, Meng came down to work with chains on his ankles. After about two weeks they removed the chains and allowed him to move about as before.

A New Colleague

After several months in the prison the guards no longer made me go upstairs at night but allowed me to sleep in the workroom. While this meant they trusted me more, I knew I still had to be very cautious.

The first time I did not join my other companions upstairs to sleep it was clear they had been worried about me. The next morning, I asked permission from the room guard to go to the carpenters' workshop under the pretext of making a picture frame, in order to get some news. The carpenters all looked up when I came in and Tuon looked relieved to see me. Uncle Kong shook his head slightly and said:

"Why didn't you go to sleep last night? I was very worried and imagined all sorts of things had happened to you. I was glad to see you painting this morning. What did you do last night?"

"They told me to sleep in the workroom, Uncle. They said it was the order from the prison chief."

I asked Tuon if he had any news. He looked around and said: "I don't really know what's going on. But more and more prisoners are coming in. The prison is almost full now. I am worried that when they bring new ones in they will take the old ones out. You must also be careful."

I returned to my workroom. On the way I saw two European men being led blind-folded and handcuffed, wearing only underwear. Oh God! They lived overseas across the horizon, but they were caught and tortured here too? I didn't dare to look long at them and continued to my workroom.

After the room guard went out to eat lunch, I told my friends about the European people but they did not believe me. They said I was just joking to ease the tension. But just then the prison guards walked the two Europeans past the window of our room across the prison yard towards Building C.

Tuoch shook his head and sighed deeply. "Where did they take these men from? That's the end now!" he said.

From day to day, I tried to focus on my work and not be careless although I secretly gave Meng cigarettes when the room guards were out. I had been warned to be careful by Tuoch and Khun, but Meng was the first person I had met when I arrived. Even though there were strict, life-threatening restrictions, I had to take the risk because I felt so sorry for him.

One day I received news from a guard who used to come and watch me painting pictures.

"Hey, do you know the wood sculptor? He has a diploma from the fine arts school in Phnom Penh."

I wasn't sure how to answer his no-head-or-tail question and feared a trick. I told him I did not know much about Phnom Penh. After the guard left, we looked at each other doubtfully. Khun said softly that it would not be long before we had another workmate. We figured there must be a new prisoner who was also a wood sculptor. I asked Khun if he had known that a new painter was coming before I was sent to work with them.

"Yes, I did. I heard them talking about that. But I didn't know why they would send a new painter here. There were plenty of painters here and they had already sent a few painters down before but not for long. Most were sent away after a couple of days."

I felt a chill in my backbone and knew I was lucky to have survived.

"Why were the others sent back?" I asked.

"Because they could not do the work. They only knew a little bit. They had been brought here as an experiment."

Another week passed, then more than a month, and still the newcomer had not arrived. One day about 9 a.m., Deuch and two bodyguards came to my room as usual. We stood up to show our respect and Deuch nodded. He gazed at my painting, and turned to look at the sculptures without uttering a word although he looked satisfied. Then he sat down quietly on the sofa in the corner of the room. My friends and I continued our work as usual and the room turned silent.

Then Deuch said, "Comrade Peng! Have you ordered him in?"

"Yes, I have already sent someone to get him," Peng answered, lowering his head slightly in deference.

A few moments later, two prison guards walked a blindfolded prisoner into the workroom. Thin and pale, he was handcuffed and his hair grew over his shoulders.

"Release him!" Deuch ordered. "How old are you?"

"I'm 42 years old," the prisoner answered.

"What region are you from? Why were you arrested?" Deuch continued.

"The northwestern region of Siem Reap. I don't know why I was arrested."

"Damn you! Speaking to me, you must be a bit gentle. Sit with your legs folded!"

I was startled to hear such harsh words. When they brought me down, Deuch did not use such brutal language. I continued listening carefully.

"You learned at the fine arts school. You know that guy?" Deuch said, pointing at Tuoch.

"No, I don't know him," the prisoner replied.

"So what is your name?" Deuch asked, softening his voice a little.

"My name is Chan."

"Okay, Comrade Peng, take his handcuffs off!"

Peng signaled the two guards to remove the handcuffs and Chan looked around. Deuch then called on me.

"Nath! You cut the hair of your friend, okay? I will tell someone to bring you the scissors," he said. He instructed the guards to keep careful watch on Chan to make sure he didn't escape. Chan was taken to another room and locked inside. As he was led out, he looked at us pitifully.

At our meal that day, my group had a new member. I watched Chan bolting down his rice the same way I did when I first came there.

After lunch, I cut Chan's hair. It was different from my first haircut, which had been done outside by a prison guard. I was ordered to cut Chan's hair inside the locked room which meant that they did not trust Chan at all. As I combed his hair, lice dropped like sesame seeds. I could not help laughing. Chan asked me why I was laughing.

I told my new friend: "I laugh, because you are not different from me. My hair was full of lice. I laughed because we are artists and we have both gone through this same day. I don't know how to cut hair, but I did not dare to protest when they ordered me to do so. We'll just make it shorter."

After I finished, the room guard ordered me to take Chan to have a wash. When I first came downstairs, the guard ordered Meng to watch me washing myself. Now, I was watching Chan. So, in the future, who would Chan watch?

New Iron Doors

The days moved forward endlessly, with my work continuing to receive good results. Every day, Deuch would bring different people to watch us working. They were very interested in Tuoch's and Khun's sculptures. Deuch seemed to take good care of the new visitors who came in, both in how he treated them and how he spoke to them. This implied that those people were not of a low rank. Chan, who had just started with us, was kept very busy.

Every day, the room guard would take him to the workshop to make tools for sculpting. Chan was cursed and threatened by the room guard almost every day because he was bored of taking Chan up and down to the workshop. Did they think that ours were easy jobs? We had spent years to learn these skills for life-long careers that were peaceful and clean, while the guards' only skills were to pull a trigger to kill people and destroy things according to their slogans broadcast on the radio every day: "Everything from the previous regime must be destroyed ... Build a new Kampuchea prosperous and progressive with great leaps."

It had been nearly one week since Chan had come downstairs. After we finished working at night, the room guard took him back to sleep in another room. I wanted to act in a friendly manner with Chan and ask him about himself but there was no convenient time to do so. We just met during meals. All I could do was try to give him spiritual strength, to make him feel that he was not alone, and that there were friends around him.

One morning shortly after I got to work, carpenters came in and quietly measured all the windows of our workroom as well as the door of Chan's room. We looked at each other doubtfully after they left.

About an hour later, the carpenters came back with drills, metal doors and iron bars for the windows. They welded a new door to the workroom and replaced the door of Chan's room as well. When the room guard went out for lunch, we began to discuss what was happening.

"The situation outside must have changed," I said. "That's why they are being so careful with us."

"That's probably right," Khun said.

We looked at Chan's room, where he stared back quietly from inside.

Tuoch put out his theory: "They don't trust us because there are a lot of us now. So, they have to make a cage for us."

After lunch, we continued our work as the carpenters returned to continue welding the iron doors and windows. One of the workers was a middle-aged man whose skill was welding iron. They called him "Ta Dek," or Iron Granddad. When the room guard was not paying too much attention, he moved to whisper to Khun. The look on Khun's face changed several times as they talked. I understood immediately that there must be something happening. Afterwards Khun continued working as normal but shot me a quick look, making me feel very curious.

As soon as the room guard left for dinner, Khun told me the news.

"Brother Pech was beaten until he was unconscious this morning while he was working."

I listened to Khun with a saddened heart. I felt much pity for Pech, who was a machinery engineer. He was a friendly person and had sent cigarettes through me to Meng. What was he guilty of? Each time I met him, he would always remind me to be careful. He worked very hard, because he was afraid of the prison cadre. But in the end he could not get away from their maltreatment.

I felt very confused. I was worried about the fact that they had put in the iron doors and windows. And now a friend of mine had been beaten badly.

Eastern Zone Purges

As far as I knew, it had been more than five months since I first came down to work. I'd painted eight portraits of Pol Pot.

Then Deuch ordered me to work with the stone sculptor. Four of us were responsible for molding statues of Pol Pot out of concrete for about four months. In fact I had never learned sculpting skills but they thought I would be better at it than those who knew nothing about art.

The prison began to get busier. Hundreds of prisoners in long lines were brought into Tuol Sleng day and night and trucks came and went endlessly. Why were they detaining so many people, I wondered. Some big event must be happening outside. I didn't dare ask anyone. When I was upstairs I could get information from the carpenter, but the downstairs roommates did not know what was going on.

The new prisoners appeared to all be soldiers. Most were not kept for very long, only a day or two. Sometimes they were sent straight upstairs upon arrival. Soon we'd see them coming down wearing only underpants, handcuffed to each other in long lines. They were blindfolded and dragged back to the trucks in which they'd arrived. Where were they being taken?

One day a young guard came and stood next to me, watching me make the sculpture molds. I asked him lightly: "Brother, you must be very tired these days. I see you all working so hard, both day and night?"

"Er, yes, of course," said the guard. He glanced over his shoulder and continued: "Those Eastern Zone traitors wanted to betray us. Now the traitor So Phim who wanted to flee to Vietnam has already been destroyed by *Angkar* and all of his links have been arrested."

"So, all of those newcomers are So Phimists, Brother?" I asked.

"Why should we spare them, the traitors!" the guard answered.

So that was it. So Phim was the Khmer Rouge chief in charge of the Eastern Zone of Cambodia. If So Phim had betrayed them, why hadn't they killed only him and his men? Why were they killing tens of thousands of other people? It was exactly like the proverb: "To dig up grass you have to dig up the roots as well." I had the feeling that an even bigger event was coming up.

The days moved forward. On July 15, 1978 they let the workmen rest for three days, not telling us why. They took us all to the upstairs room where I used to stay before. All of us felt uneasy, not understanding what was going on. I got close to the carpenter again.

"Uncle, I've heard that So Phim has betrayed the Khmer Rouge and the prisoners coming in every day are all soldiers from the Eastern Region. Is that true?" I asked.

"Probably yes. I've heard the same thing downstairs," he answered.

"But why are they putting us up here to sleep and eat. Maybe it's not safe, Uncle?"

"Ha! Nephew, don't think too much. Just remember the goodness of our mothers and fathers. It's useless to think about this. Whenever we die, we die," he responded.

Day by day, the noise of arriving trucks increased in front of the prison. During the last month, especially since we'd been taken upstairs, the numbers of prisoners entering Tuol Sleng had increased. Some of the prisoners didn't realize where they were going because they had come with their bags of clothes, which were piled in a mountain near my workroom. Some were just children, only ten years old.

"Uncle," I said, "This time, it seems the Khmer race must be vanishing. Do you know where they are taking the prisoners with their hands in handcuffs and their faces blindfolded?"

"I think they are taking them off to kill them," he responded.

"Kill them! Where could they be taking so many people to kill?"

"I told you already that Peng had us sharpen eight machetes. Then the other day, I saw one of the men carrying a bunch of bloody handcuffs to clean in the water jar. It was unbelievable."

"Oh God! What are they doing this for? Thousands, tens of thousands of people have been killed."

I had heard that during the Second World War the Germans killed millions of people. But the Germans did not kill only the German people. Why were the Khmers eliminating their own race?

Three days passed, and we came to work as usual. Four of us, including Meng, were preparing the molds for a statue of Brother Number One: Pol Pot. We worked carefully, hoping for good results when we opened the molds in a few days. We were lucky when we opened it up to find the statue unscratched and in good shape. Deuch and his colleagues had big smiles on their faces.

Later *Angkar* had a plan to produce statues from silver. Deuch sent his men to go out and collect thousands of kilos of silver items to make solid silver statues. First we had to adjust all the molds so they looked exactly like Pol Pot.

Then all of us were entrusted with a new job: to make an eight-meter-tall concrete statue of Pol Pot standing with farmers carrying flags and such — intended to show the history of the class struggle. It was to be constructed on the top of Wat Phnom and the Buddhist stupa and pagodas there would be torn down. First we made a small model of the statue to send to Pol Pot for his approval.

Final Days

During August and September 1978, the prison gradually quieted down. Not many new prisoners came in, although the guards continued to take old prisoners out in trucks every day. In September a very strange thing happened. They began to put most of the prison guards in custody. I didn't know what they were guilty of. I guessed that they had been charged with having links with people whom *Angkar* considered enemies, such as So Phim in the East, Koy Thuon in the North, Khek Pen in the Northwest, or they were ministers within the Party Center such as Vorn Vet and Cheng An. When those people were arrested, they had to search for every single link down to the lower levels. Many people died because of innocent associations with the accused.

On September 30, *Angkar* celebrated a festival throughout the country to commemorate the day that *Angkar* officially and openly declared itself dedicated to communism. The festival went on for three days. During this time, Deuch and the guards did not come into our room because they were busy with the festival.

After the September 30 festival had been over for a week, the prison guards began to renovate the entire prison. They pulled down the barbed wire from three of the buildings — A, B, and D — knocked down the small cells on the first two floors, and demolished the walls on the top floor. On the ground floor of Building A, they rebuilt and painted the small cells. Only Building C was left untouched.

My friends and I became worried, assuming that they were going to discontinue use of S-21 as a prison, especially since there had not been any new prisoners during the last several days. There were only a few old prisoners left in Building C. The bustle and activity of the September 30 festival was over, and the place turned silent, with only a few guards remaining in the prison. The guards no longer came by to look at the sculptures. If the prison shut down, what would become of us?

One day, I was absorbed in my work and looked up to see the shadow of a person standing at the window, looking at me with one eye. The room guard was asleep in the corner of the room, snoring loudly. I wanted to wake him but didn't dare. I knew he was in big trouble this time, because the one-eyed man was Hor, the chief of the prison military unit. Hor rarely came to watch me work, and I wondered why he was standing so long at the window. Entering the room, he saw that the room guard was sleeping. All of us jumped off our stools to show respect to Hor, and I moved towards the guard to wake him up.

"Don't wake him. Let him sleep!" the military chief said. The guard opened his eyes and immediately jumped up, but it was too late.

"You, comrade, go and find a place to sleep," Hor said. The room guard just stood there, his face pale. "I told you to go find a place to sleep. Are you deaf?" Hor shouted. These last words made me shiver. The room guard walked out without saying a word. Hor sat down on the sofa and crossed his legs. He sat quietly for a moment. I felt worried and frightened, looking at my colleagues' faces.

Finally Hor said with a laugh, "Hey guys, let me ask you something. Have you ever thought of leaving this place, or going out to farm?"

I was extremely careful not to make a wrong move, or say the wrong thing. This guy rarely came here. Why was he asking this question out of the blue? It was clear from the way he was laughing that we must answer. We looked at each other, unsure, wanting to say the right thing but not daring to speak. Hor continued laughing. The atmosphere became unbearable. We all felt like people who had lost their souls. Unable to stand it any longer, I burst out without thinking: "Yes, Brother! I've already decided to live under the guidance of *Angkar*. Whatever direction *Angkar* sends me, I'm committed to staying there."

"Oh really? How about Meng and Tuoch?"

They both agreed.

"Okay, continue your work!"

The tension subsided but I still had no idea why he had come to ask us this question. Then Hor stood up and walked away. I turned to my friends.

"Why did he come and ask us this? Or is this the last day of our lives?"

"Hard to guess," Tuoch said. "As we've seen, they've not brought in more prisoners. So maybe we have to leave this place."

"Oh mother's milk, help your sons now," Tuoch said, raising his joined palms to the sky.

"Everything depends on God," I said. "This is our last hope."

I looked through the window for the room guards, but none of them were around. After a while they sent a new person to replace the room guard that Hor had sent away — perhaps to his death.

Days and months passed by endlessly. The entire prison became a bit more busy. The guards moved the prisoners in Building A from upstairs to the new cells on the ground floor. But there were not as many prisoners in there as before, only about 10. I'd heard the guards call these new cells in Building A the "special prison," where special persons with high ranks were detained. Afterward I learned they put only one person in each room, with a proper bed, but with a shackle on their ankles. The special prisoners seemed to get adequate food rations and careful attention was paid to their security. Guards slept in hammocks in front of the doors to their rooms.

By December 1978 almost everything was different in the prison. The guards no longer cooked for us and brought our meals to us. They let one of us go out to cook our own food in a shed outside. The constant smoke and flames from the stoves for cooking for the prisoners also died down. I guessed that there were only about 10 or 20 prisoners shackled in the rooms.

Every once in a while we heard the sounds of artillery and gunfire in the distance. The sounds of people screaming from pain had also disappeared. Now we only heard wind making the shutters bang against the walls. I was still working on the large sculpture about the party struggle. The previous week they took the model of the sculpture to Pol Pot for his approval, but I didn't know what the result was.

One day I went to cook lunch in the wooden shed as usual. It seemed extremely quiet when I got there, making me feel apprehensive. Why was it so quiet? Where had all the carpenters gone? Only Tuon and a few others were still there. Tuon moved close to me and said:

"Brother, you know last night they took more than 10 workers out, but they haven't come back yet. I bet they don't return. What are we going to do?"

Tuon looked very frightened, and my hands and feet turned cold.

"Who did they take?" I asked quietly. Tuon told me the names of the blacksmiths, electricians, and carpenters who had disappeared.

"It won't be long for me and the others," he said.

I felt sick and it was hard to concentrate on cooking. When I finished I went back to the workroom. The guards had all gone to lunch so I took the opportunity to tell my friends the news. We were all very frightened. That night I couldn't sleep. I lay my hand across my forehead thinking of when they would take me off to kill me, and of my wife and children back in our home village. I raised my hands and prayed to the good deeds of Lord Buddha and that of my parents, to help save my life.

In the distance I could hear the sound of artillery more often, day and night. But this night the sound of the big guns stirred my heart to feel brave and even a little hopeful. It was more than a year since I had been arrested. Many times I'd felt panic that I was going to be killed. Why was I still frightened? I tried to rein in my feelings but couldn't. Had the heroes who dared to sacrifice their lives for their country or for honor felt such panic? Nobody but the heroes knew this.

It got deeper into the night and the prison compound became deadly quiet. There was only the wind blowing, bringing along the coldness that made us feel a chill in the backbone. On the tops of the trees, the lonely sound of the night doves crying made me feel goosebumps all over my body. I grabbed an old blanket to cover myself, and tried to close my eyes until I fell asleep, frightened.

Escape

On January 7, 1979, I woke early and went to work as usual. The prison was quiet, even peaceful. Only a few prisoners remained in Building A. The guards were hanging their hammocks and napping. Around 11 o'clock I asked permission from the room guard to go cook lunch, as usual. At the wooden shed I saw Tuon, who seemed happy because he had a large bowl of fresh fish.

"Don't you know, Brother?" he said. "Last night they called me out in the heart of the night. I was so frightened my soul almost disappeared. But when we got outside, they told me to cut fish heads all night long."

I was also happy; we rarely had such good food as we had on that day. While I was cleaning the rice we heard successive explosions, artillery shelling along with small arms fire. I set the cooking pot down and ran over to Tuon.

"Brother, why is the gunfire so loud," I said. "It's like it's on the main street near here."

Tuon didn't reply but crouched next to me. At the same time the guards were running here and there about the prison yard. The alarm bells began to ring, signaling the guards to gather. I turned and saw my room guard running towards me.

"Painter, come; come quickly!"

I ran back to my workroom; the other workmen were already there. The guard locked the door from the outside and ran off. My friends and I looked at each other's faces with the sense that it was our turn now. We could hear more and more gunfire and nothing else. A while later the door of the room was opened and Tuon and several other craftsmen were pushed inside.

"You guys stay still and don't make any noise. Be careful," the guards said while banging the shutters closed. We all sat sadly, looking at each other without saying a word. I realized the critical moment had come. We didn't know whether they would spare our lives or not. We could hear louder and more frequent gunfire outside.

An hour later, we heard the footsteps of someone running erratically outside the room. The door flew open, revealing two guards carrying AK-47s.

"Get out, all of you guys!" one of them shouted.

We stood up and filed out of the room. I tried to hold in my feelings so as not to have too much panic. Outside, some of the guards were already standing there waiting for us with their guns in their hands.

"Walk in a straight line! We will shoot and kill you guys if you dare step out of line!"

These rough words together with their cruel faces made our spirits sink. They threatened us and loaded bullets into the guns. Without delay, a line of 13 people started moving forward under their orders.

As we filed out of the prison, we knew there was no way we could escape. Armed men carrying loaded guns were walking on both sides of us. If we dared to rush out one step, there wouldn't be another step. So we didn't care where they were taking us.

Outside the prison compound, I saw Deuch and a few guards — some standing and others sitting — with guns in their hands ready for combat. The procession of prisoners turned toward a building on the western corner of the prison. They put all of us in a house and locked it from the outside.

"Sleep quietly and don't make any noise," one of the guards said, leaning through the window and then closing the shutters. Outside we could hear the constant noise of gunfire. I moved to Tuon and whispered:

"Brother, do you have any hope that they will spare our lives?"

"Hard to know what's going on," Tuon said.

"But if they would kill us, why did they take us outside?"

"It's hard for me to trust this, because they are behaving so brutally."

Frightened and exhausted from having nothing in my stomach, I lay down by Tuon and fell asleep. Later we were awakened by someone ordering us to move out. We all rushed out in a line, as the guards led us south through the city streets. They were very careful each time we crossed the main avenues. We went through Tuol Tompong market and then headed west.

Around 5 o'clock in the afternoon we arrived at a small house in a sugarcane field outside of Phnom Penh. I began to believe that they would not kill us because there were many other people there, including the families of Deuch and the guards. Young and old, the group totaled about 100. The noise of gunfire had died down a bit.

About an hour later, all the people started walking west through the sugarcane fields. Tuon and I were ordered to carry rice. We struggled to carry a half sack of rice between the two of us. After we had walked a bit we heard jet fighter planes flying above. The guards shouted out for everyone to hide, as anti-aircraft guns made a deafening roar. Tuon and I did not run far because we did not dare leave the sack of rice behind.

Night fell and the procession was still moving forward. I couldn't see well and fell off an embankment into a pit, spraining my ankle. I could hardly move my body from the pain. One of the guys standing on the embankment pointed his gun at me and said:

"Now, can you get up or not?"

Feeling frightened and with Tuon's help I lifted myself up. Tuon called another man to help him carry the rice. I continued walking behind the others, limping because of the swollen ankle.

From all directions the artillery was turned on Phnom Penh. We were told that the Vietnamese were attacking and that the Khmer Rouge were destroying them, but the shells were falling on the capital. Turning back I saw huge blazes all over the city, with bombs and shells exploding like popcorn being roasted. We could feel the tremor of tanks shaking the earth. More and more people were appearing. The people I had been with earlier in the day had all disappeared and I was now surrounded by people I didn't know. I followed them slowly but suddenly there was a stampede and I was pushed to the ground. I scrambled to get up, but when I regained my feet I found that everyone had gone. I walked back slowly the way we'd come and found a bag of rice and baggage scattered all over the rice fields. I hoisted the rice bag onto my shoulder and limped on. A while later, I found the same crowds of people I'd just met. Exhausted and thirsty I sat down near them. After a few minutes, they got up in a group and continued walking and I went with them. After about 10 meters I saw a man sitting with his hands covering his head. He was moaning with pain. I recognized his voice: it was Kong, who worked as a carpenter with Tuon in the prison.

"Uncle, what's the matter with you?" I asked quietly.

"Oh nephew, the crowd ran over me and almost killed me when they panicked and ran. We've all separated. Help me!"

I lifted him up and put his arm around my neck, walking him forward slowly.

"Uncle, have you seen Tuon?" I asked.

"We were walking together before the crowd panicked, but I don't know where he's gone now."

He told me we were near Prey Sar. I'd heard of the place but didn't know exactly where it was. If we tried to slip off now it would be no good because I didn't know where to go. And we'd be really unlucky if we came across the prison guards. So we limped along through the night, arm in arm until the horizon began to shine vaguely; it was nearly dawn. The crowds of people continued to move forward. I looked back at Phnom Penh every once in a while and saw bright lights all over the capital. We could still hear gunfire and explosions.

As the day became brighter, I began looking for my friends from the prison and found Tuon. I gave half of the rice to him in case we got separated again. He didn't know where our other friends were. The sky was light now and the three of us continued along, with Kong able to walk by himself now. Thousands of people were crowded together on the road. Suddenly we saw the prison guard Peng and his colleagues standing by a railroad track.

"Tuon! Come over here!" Peng called. As Tuon walked to them Kong and I sped forward. I looked back and saw Tuon talking to the guards until the crowds of people blocked our view. I never saw Tuon again.

Kong and I went ahead without knowing where we were going.

The sun was now shining brightly in the sky. It was January 8, 1979. Later in the morning, I saw Pech and Chan from the prison, each of them carrying a hen in their hands. I hurried towards them, calling out for them to wait for me. We'd now formed a group of four. I looked back for Tuon but it was no use. I didn't even see his shadow.

"Brothers, there are now only four of us left, so let's make sure we don't get separated again," I said, grabbing a cooking pot I saw by the side of the road. It was now 8 o'clock and we had arrived at a hill of watermelons. There were about 50 people sitting there eating watermelons. We were hungry and thirsty so we headed over. Unfortunately I saw my room guard, sitting with three or four prisoners from my group.

"Where are the others?" he asked.

"They got lost," I responded.

I looked around and saw Meng, Tuoch and three other carpenters, as well as three other prison guards with their AK-47 rifles.

"Eat these watermelons first," the guard said. "We have only this place to cross and then we will be free from danger."

I barely took notice of his words, staring at the watermelons. One of the guards noticed my swollen foot.

"Hey guy, your foot is so swollen. Can you run fast if there is any problem?" he asked.

I played it down, telling him that I'd had to run on it last night. In fact I was hurting badly, but I would have to use some tricks or they would finish me off. After eating, we were ready to cross Route 4. It was about 200 meters from the watermelon field to the national road. We stood up and started walking, with the four guards following. Looking back I saw crowds of people coming along behind us. The stronger ones had already reached the road, while my friends and I had another 100 meters to go. Suddenly five trucks and a jeep with a red flag showing the yellow form of Angkor Wat drove up from the east.

"Who do those trucks belong to!" I shouted out to the prison guards.

The guards were bewildered. We heard gunfire and soldiers began piling out of the trucks as bullets flew above our heads. The four of us turned back, jumping into a nearby pit. The guards had already disappeared. Chan and I ran with our heads lowered until we got to a bamboo grove near the watermelon field. There we lay down on the ground, looking towards the road. We saw soldiers walking all over the road. About two hours later the gunfire died down. The crowds of people trying to cross the road had disappeared, as had the soldiers. I inched towards Chan.

"Hey Brother! What shall we do? They've all run away."

Chan didn't answer. I walked over to the pit, where I was relieved to find Kong and Pech still hiding. We went back to the watermelon field. Luckily enough I had some rice and the cooking pot. We cooked the rice and roasted a chicken right there.

It was now three o'clock in the afternoon. After eating we rested to regain our strength, keeping an eye on the highway in case anyone should come along. We decided to follow the highway back to Phnom Penh. It was already four o'clock and we decided to head off soon.

As soon as we started walking on the highway we felt hopeful that we would survive and might be able to enjoy freedom again. Trucks carrying soldiers passed us by without incident, making me feel more confident. A smile appeared on my face again. The four of walked together with a few other families heading in the same direction — to Phnom Penh.

We spent two days and two nights on the 32-kilometer long road before we arrived in Phnom Penh. Along the way Pech found a cart to carry the rice and cooking pot.

When we arrived at the road heading to the Tuol Kork section on the outskirts of Phnom Penh, the liberating soldiers welcomed us warmly. This was the day the four of us finally had complete freedom. The others also looked jubilant and smiled from their hearts. I felt like shouting out to the sky to say that I had survived and finally had freedom.

Three days later the four of us had to move ahead because more and more people were coming into Phnom Penh. The four of us pushed the cart across the quiet Phnom Penh streets, where rubbish was scattered about, blown by the wind. We passed burned trucks and tanks turned upside down. We walked along Norodom Boulevard to the intersection of Chinese Hospital, and then turned toward Independence Monument. We went straight to the riverside to look for a place to cook rice.

At that time, it seemed there were only four of us making the trip across Phnom Penh. All the houses on the streets were closed, and some of them were covered with overgrown grass and brush. The city looked desolate.

We lived on our bag of rice for a week and then went to Wat Phnom to receive donated rice from the Foodstuff Distributing Committee. From then on, I tried to ask people about my family in my home village. But no one had any news about them.

Reunion

On February 3, 1979, my three friends and I volunteered to join Division 1 of the new Cambodian army, which had been installed by the Vietnamese to defend Phnom Penh. After several months I got permission from my commander to search for my family in Battambang. The direct route via Highway Five was not yet secure, so I hitchhiked around the Tonle Sap lake on Highway Six. It took me four days and four nights to reach Battambang.

Upon arriving in Battambang town I immediately asked a crowd of people if they had any news of my family. None of them knew anything and instead I became the focus, as they plied me with questions about the situation in Phnom Penh. After an hour I was able to pull myself away. The sun was already low as I hurried the four kilometers to my home village. As I crossed the concrete bridge over the river I remembered the events of four years ago, when soldiers had fired into the air to stop me and others from crossing and killed a government soldier on the spot. But now I could enjoy full freedom. The bridge was open on both sides.

I walked across the bridge, my heart thumping, speeding up the closer I got to my village. Arriving at the village I looked around for familiar faces but found none. I felt very strange and unsettled. Where had my neighbors gone? I only saw the strange faces of new settlers. All the large houses had disappeared, replaced by ramshackle huts. Even my house was not there any more, not even its shadow. There was only overgrown grass and brush. I felt despondent and exhausted and turned toward a nearby cottage. The owner was my former neighbor and I knew him very well. I asked for news of my family.

"Nath," he said, "After you were arrested your children got sick and died one by one. Your grand aunt also died, from starvation."

My knees weakened and I dropped to the ground, my tears flowing soundlessly.

"How about my wife? Where is she?" I asked.

"I'm not sure. Go to your brother's house. He may know about her."

I walked to several nearby cottages built on a hill in the middle of the rice field, where I met my brothers and sisters, nephews and nieces. I was choked and stifled, unable to speak, with my tears falling instead. I tried to pull in my sorrow as my relatives and neighbors gathered around me. They all thought I had died.

"I never thought I'd see you again," my brother said. "Last month the people held a ceremony to commemorate the spirits of the people who had died. I commemorated your spirit then. Since you were arrested we had not heard any news from you."

I asked my brother to take me to see my wife, who I was told lived about three kilometers away. As we walked I listened to my brother's news. The sky was getting dark as he pointed to a small cottage in front of us.

"There! Your wife's cottage."

Sitting alone in the doorway of her house in the shade of a tamarind tree, my wife didn't recognize me until I was five steps away. "Eng!" I called with a shaky voice. She looked up, finally recognizing me, and called out my name. We embraced each other without saying a word. Nothing could hold our tears back and neither of us noticed the people flocking around us. For the first hour I couldn't say anything; my wife just cried as she told me that both of our sons had died. After dinner and throughout the night, I listened to my wife telling the story of what happened to her and my children after I was arrested. In the morning I went to see the graves of my children. Recalling the painful stories made me unable to hold back my tears as I cleaned the grass around their graves. When I was taken away in December 1977 my older son was nearly five but the younger was only six months old.

A couple days later, I heard that Luom, the man who arrested me, was living not far from my village. After he heard that I had returned, he never dared to sleep at home and only returned for meals because he was afraid I would take revenge on him. Hearing this, I decided my wife and I would go to his house one evening at dinner time. As soon as Luom saw me the expression changed on his face. After we managed to sit down Luom spoke first before I could say anything.

"Brother, at that time I didn't know anything," he said. "They ordered me to go and call you at the rice field, and I just followed that. I didn't know that they were about to arrest you."

I interrupted him: "Luom, listen to me. For all the things that have passed, I never thought of taking revenge or showering my anger on anyone. Especially you, Luom. Don't think that I would do anything against you. What happened then was not your idea or your fault. We were just tools for them to use. In the past, we were innocent people, clean farmers who made our living peacefully. We would help each other when in need. Now, we have survived and that is our great luck."

Luom's face turned fresh again. His wife invited us for dinner, but we just thanked them and went back home.

Return to Tuol Sleng

At the end of August 1979, I brought my wife to Phnom Penh and continued my work with the military. In November the government asked me and several other survivors to help organize a Museum of Genocide on the grounds of the prison. The idea of returning to that horrifying place filled me with dread but it was my decision to return. I worked as a painter there, preparing scenes of life in S-21 to let Cambodians and visitors from other countries know what had happened.

On my first day back I tried to distance myself from my feelings so that I wouldn't be overcome with sadness. I kept reminding myself that I was enjoying my freedom now, and that the frightening days were gone. As I entered the prison compound I had an indescribable feeling. The place was very quiet, but full of rubbish everywhere because no one was living there. Prisoner records were scattered all the way from the entrance to the office. Everything looked exactly the same as before. Nothing had changed; all four buildings were there. The electric fence made of corrugated iron sheets and barbed wire was still in place. My friends and I walked around and quietly picked up the documents, putting them into one pile. I kept looking at Building D, the building where I had been shackled and almost starved to death; the place where I had completely lost all hope in life. I could hardly believe that I was standing there now. As I fell deep into this feeling, I heard one of my friends calling me from behind.

"Nath! What are you looking at?" Uncle Kong, one my four friends, asked me.

"Uncle, we should not come back here! No, we should not!" In my mind, I felt that I was still a prisoner there.

"I feel the same as you do," said Kong. "Entering this place, I remember everything. But, it was something in the past … it has passed for a year now. We come here this time not blindfolded and in handcuffs. This time, we come with freedom and in a car. On the other hand, we have come here with the duty to organize this place into a museum. I believe that the spirits of the dead would be very glad about this."

On the second day, I did not feel as anxious about being on the old prison grounds. What surprised us was to notice the graves in front of Building A. When were these graves dug up? January 7 was the last day I had been there. There were no graves then. I asked some of the other people working there and they told me that about a week after January 7, the liberating Khmer and Vietnamese soldiers launched a clean-up attack there and found these bodies on the beds in Building A. The corpses were swelling and rotten, and were buried there in the yard. The military had also taken photographs for the record.

I guessed that the graves were of special prisoners who had been high-ranking Khmer Rouge cadre. When the guards ordered us out at gunpoint, those people were still there, alive. They must have killed these people after we had left. It was pitiful that they could survive until that final day, but didn't have the luck to live past that.

After a discussion to allocate tasks, I was given the responsibility to paint pictures and found a quiet room on the second floor of one of the buildings in which to work. Pech was appointed as service director responsible for the general work there and Uncle Kong was put in charge of carpentry.

Two months later, on January 7, 1980, the Tuol Sleng Genocide Museum was opened to the public. Both Khmer and foreign visitors were shocked by the brutality that appeared in photographs, paintings, and from torture tools on display. In some cases, we heard the cries of horrified visitors who saw the pictures of their husbands, wives, or children who had been killed here.

"I've been separated from my family for ten years," cried one woman, after seeing the photograph of her husband and son. "I have been trying to search for news about them. And finally, I have just found out now."

She was not the only person who was trapped in this misery. This sad story occurred frequently because Tuol Sleng was an official prison of the People's Central Committee from all levels. Prisoners such as teachers, physicians, soldiers, Khmer Rouge cadre, and civil servants from the Lon Nol regime were all taken here from all the provinces throughout the country. What they shared was that they were suspected of having tendencies or links with the previous government.

Meeting Sor

One month passed, and I felt pleased with what I had contributed so far. Crowds of people came to visit the museum every day except on Monday, when employees had a day off work. One day, I went to work as usual, but I was a bit late. At the gate of the prison I saw people already crowding in. I got off my bicycle, walked it through the crowd, and looked around a moment. Suddenly I felt suspicious of a person covering his face with a *krahma*. I looked carefully at him again and was completely startled. I left my bicycle and rushed to Pech.

"Brother, I saw Sor in line — just outside there."

Sor had been a security guard in this prison. He was also a barber, because when they removed the shackles from me he was ordered by Deuch to cut my hair. I was then very afraid of him. Why had he come back here?

I rushed back out with Pech, Chan, and Kong following me. Once we were outside, I took a glance around and spotted Sor immediately. I walked up to him, blocked his way, and greeted him by name.

"No, my name is not Sor," he said, his face still covered. "You must be mistaken."

I seized him by his wrist and pulled the *krahma* away, revealing his pale face, which we quickly recognized even though we had not seen him for a year.

"Sor, don't be afraid, because I won't do you any harm. I only want to ask you something."

I took him inside the gate to the museum sitting room and closed the door, with my friends following.

"Why did you come here?" I asked.

"Did you come to study the situation?" Pech echoed my question.

"No, Brother!" he said. "I came to visit Phnom Penh with other people, and came here because it is said to be interesting and we could have fun here. I wanted to go back this morning, but my friends took me to visit this place. I didn't expect that anyone here would recognize me."

Chan was quiet for a while and then asked Sor where he now lived.

"I live in Kbal Koh village, Sa'ang district."

"And where were you on January 7?"

"I was at Prey Sar. I had been transferred there nearly half a year." This was probably true, because I hadn't seen him for a long time.

"When did you start work in this prison?"

"1976."

"You worked here for a long time. So, you must have known many things," Chan said. "Now, I want to know one thing: were any prisoners ever released by *Angkar* since you worked here?

"No, never. All the prisoners here were to be executed without having a chance to go back. Not even one."

As I listened to him, I looked at Pech, Chan, and Kong, thinking of our luck in being able to get away from such a hell with our lives. Chan continued the interrogation.

"How many people did you kill?"

"I never killed anyone."

"How can I believe you — you were among the killers!"

"No! There was a group of killers: it was a hot and destructive group. This group was among the security guards under the control of A-Pech, A-Bou and A-Huy."

"How dare you call the three guards 'A'?" I interrupted. "A" is used in Khmer in front of the name of an inferior or despicable person.

Sor looked at me briefly and then looked at the ground like a monkey afraid of his master. I asked the others if they had any more questions for Sor.

"I want to know why you didn't run away with the Khmer Rouge and instead went back to your village," Uncle Kong asked reluctantly, in the manner of an old man.

"When things were in chaos, I was at Prey Sar. When the others ran away, I escaped from them that night, January 7, and went to my village because I missed my parents so much."

"From January 7 until now, have you seen anyone who used to work with you?" I asked.

"I have never seen anyone since that day, because I tried to hide myself and helped my parents with their farming. On the other hand, nobody in the village knew I used to work here."

"Do you know where the others are now?"

"No, I don't. I just knew that they were going to the west."

"All right, now," Pech said. "The sun is already a bit high. I think this is enough. You can go. There's more that I want to know, but there's not enough time right now. And you also don't seem to know the important things clearly. You were just a junior security guard even though you used to sometimes do inhumane acts towards the prisoners. It has already passed. You can go back home freely."

We knew that if we had taken Sor outside and told the crowds that he was a former guard that he would have been killed instantly. But we were not seeking revenge, and let him go. Sor took his leave, looking like a soulless man. I never saw him again, even though I tried to find him later at Kbal Koh village.

The Ghost List

During my first year at the museum, I was given free rein to work on my paintings, achieving a certain serenity through my work. I began to believe that the spirits of the people who died there would be able to rest in peace. Sometimes we invited monks to come and hold ceremonies at the prison in commemoration of the dead.

One day, at about one o'clock in the afternoon, a staffperson who was researching the prison documents called me over to see him on the first floor of Building B, where a group researching the records left behind in the prison worked. When I got there, he handed a piece of paper to me.

"Have a look, Brother!"

After I looked at the paper, my hands and feet became cold. It was an execution list. My name was there, but underlined in red ink with brackets at the end saying "keep." The list was signed by Sous Thy with a note written on the top: "Request Peng to destroy." The bottom of the note held the signature of Prison Chief Deuch, dated February 16, 1978. Virtually all the people who were arrested with me in Battambang and sent to Tuol Sleng with me were included on that list. After I finished reading the paper, my face grew hot and my hands and feet turned cold and shaky.

Oh God! I didn't know my name had been put on the "ghost" list for February 16, 1978. That meant that all my friends who shared the same shackles with me were killed that day. It was only at this moment that I knew clearly that none of my fellow prisoners survived.

I felt weak, as if all the bones had been taken out of my body. I returned the paper to the research group with a saddened heart, my body flooded with memories. I went out to the yard and stood gazing at the second floor of the building where we had been shackled together, somehow feeling as if those people were still alive. I used to hold hopes that some of them were still living, trapped somehow under Khmer Rouge control. When Sor told me no one had survived, I didn't believe him completely. Not until this moment did I know the truth.

Time passed and I slowly rebuilt my life. I felt much less tense, able to reveal the mystery of this prison to outsiders, so that they could know how bad it was. I believe that the spirits of the people who died must have applauded our work. Contributing to the establishment of this Genocide Museum was the most meaningful thing I had ever done. Only a handful of people who had known the taste and flavor of this prison had survived. It was my great luck that I have been born with the temperament and love for drawing and painting. If not, my name would not have been underlined in red — meaning that I was to be spared — on that February 16, 1978 "ghost" list.

A Butcher Returns

In July, 1981, I returned to my former military unit, where I worked in the artistic and cultural section. Several years passed. Even though I no longer worked at Tuol Sleng, I was often asked by foreign visitors and journalists for interviews. Sometimes they asked me to meet at Tuol Sleng. This was painful for me to do, and I sometimes refused to meet them there.

Some years later, around 1995, a number of Khmer Rouge soldiers surrendered to the government. I was told by a friend that Huy, the former butcher of Tuol Sleng, had defected to government authorities in Sa'ang district, Kandal province, where he admitted killing more than 2,000 people. A friend showed me his photograph to confirm that Huy had really been a guard at Tuol Sleng.

With one glance at the photograph, I recognized him to the bone. But when he confessed that he had killed only 2,000 people, I thought it was too few. In 1978 alone, tens of thousands of people were taken to Tuol Sleng. There were just a few guards who killed the prisoners, and Huy was one of them. So the 2,000 people he said he had killed must have been just a fraction of the total number. But no matter what he said, nobody would dare to touch him because he had defected according to the political guidelines of the government. By doing so he gained the right to live as a normal citizen and make a living.

I had told my friends that I wanted to see Huy, but I was denied any meeting with him. Maybe they were afraid I would take revenge on him. They were wrong to think so, because I had never dared to kill an animal, not to mention a human being, in my life. The reason that I wanted to see him was because I had something that I wanted to know from him. Huy had quite a high position during that regime, so he must know more than Sor. I thought he could tell me something if he did not lie to me.

After I heard about Huy's defection, I could not remain peaceful. I remembered the corpses stacked on top of each other. I could still see the guards' jubilant faces when they beat people. It was incredible that a butcher who had killed thousands of people now had the right to live happily with his wife and children. They killed people without wasting any bullets. They used wooden sticks or metal rods to smash in people's heads. Most prisoners who were taken off to be killed had already been starved and were too weak to walk or struggle with their killers. The prisoners were tied with ropes and marched in lines like cattle.

I had determined in my mind that I must meet Huy even if I had to wait for a long time. Ten years had passed since my release from Tuol Sleng and I was getting older. My friends who had survived the same prison passed away one after another. As for the museum, parts of it were collapsing or falling into disrepair. Visitors still came to the prison every day and I went there sometimes as well. The people working there were now mostly newcomers whom I had not known before, with only a few of the old staff left. My appointments were mostly with visitors from Europe or America, sometimes for a morning or a whole day.

In early 1996 I was asked to work with two French-Khmers who were preparing a documentary film about a female journalist killed at Tuol Sleng during the Pol Pot regime. I would probably be one of the actors. They asked me to paint two large pictures, one of my own story and another of the woman. During my first day with them I prepared my drawing materials, starting to draw on the second and third days, as they filmed me. They asked me to give an interview during that time.

One day as I entered the prison and walked towards the painting room, I saw the cameraman and director in the yard, aiming and panning the camera around. One of the staff walked to me and said in a low voice:

"Uncle! There — it's A-Huy! You want to see him? He's over there!"

I was startled and asked, "What? What did you say?"

"I said that A-Huy is right over there," the man stressed.

On hearing that, I felt as if all my blood had drained out. My heart stopped beating and I began shaking. Feeling weak at the knees, I sat down and looked where the man was pointing. It was Huy, dressed like a farmer and standing about ten meters from me.

It took me 15 minutes to compose myself. I was unsure if I wanted to go up to him or not. What could I say to the person I had been more afraid of than a tiger? Now suddenly he was standing right in front of me. What should I do? I tried to calm down for a moment before walking over to him, with heat coming out of my face. My palms were sticky and wet with sweat, and then they became very cold. I stopped about two meters from him and looked him in the eye. He did not notice my presence. My voice seemed very distant when I began speaking.

"You are Brother Huy, aren't you?"

A-Huy turned to me quickly and spoke in a gentle manner. "Yes, it's me," he said, turning away to watch the scenery without paying much attention to me.

He did not know that I was staring at him to the bones.

"Do you know me, Brother?" I asked.

This time, he turned to me, looked at me a bit longer, and then said, "No, I don't."

"But I know you very well. Why don't you know me? You used to be the chief of security in this prison," I said, touching his weak point.

He looked at me again and his face changed.

"No, I was only an ordinary security guard," he said.

"You've lied to me. In fact, you were the chief of the security guards here. You were responsible for transporting people in trucks to be executed at Choeung Ek," I said, raising my voice.

As I spoke, the expression on his face greatly changed. He must be wondering, I was sure, how I knew his story so well. I could see through his black heart.

"Do you recognized me? I was one of the four or five painters who worked in that room," I said pointing at our former workroom. "You used to go there often."

"At that time I was told to take the prisoners for them. How could I get away from following their orders?" he said.

"How many people did you kill?" I asked with emphasis.

" I was forced then ... I killed about four or five people, because I could not avoid doing that," he said.

I laughed and thought that even though he had turned from a cruel young man to quite an old man, his heart and mind had not changed, as none of his words were true.

"According to the reports, when you defected you confessed that you had killed more than 2,000 people. What do you think?" I asked this question to probe further, but he in turn gave me a tricky answer.

"First I told them the truth — just three or four — but they didn't believe me and they kept asking. I thought that if I told a small number, they wouldn't believe me. So I told them this big number — 2,000 — and they believed me."

I shook my head, feeling confused.

"Huy, I don't have any ill intention against you. If I did, you wouldn't be able to stand in front of me now. The reason why I keep asking you is because I just want to know. But every word you told me was a lie. When you defected, you told people that you had killed more than 2,000. The other people might believe you, because it was so impressive that you alone could kill more than 2,000 people. But I don't believe you. This number is too small for me. If I just looked at So Phim's soldiers in the Eastern Zone accused of treason, I saw them being brought in and taken out in trucks for nights on end. That number is already three or four times higher than your figure."

At this point, my mind was getting clearer. I saw him looking down at the ground. He appeared like an old sheep, very different from more than a decade ago, when he was a savage bull, a lion. None of the prisoners, including myself, had dared to look him in the face then. Now, he was in a deadlock, with no more fangs or horns. Seeing him in this situation, somehow I felt pity for him.

To avoid spoiling the atmosphere, I turned a question to him and asked if he had seen the paintings I had hung in the museum. He said he had.

"What do you think of the paintings? Are they too exaggerated?" I asked.

"No, they are not exaggerated," he said. "There were scenes more brutal than that."

"I asked because I want to know the truth. I've painted these pictures partly from what I saw and heard myself, and also from what the direct victims told me. I want you to tell the truth."

"I'm telling you the truth: It is not exaggerated," he said.

I stood still for a moment thinking over his words. Some of the scenes I had painted were what I had seen with my own eyes, scenes that depicted actual events I had witnessed. Other pictures were based on victims' descriptions. One picture — of soldiers ripping a crying baby out of an anguished mother's arms — was based on the screams and cries of women and children I had heard from within my room every couple of weeks.

"Did you see the picture of the prison guards pulling a baby away from his mother while another guy hit the mother with a stick? What did you and your men do with the babies? Where did you take them?"

"Uh ... we took them out to kill them."

"What!" I shouted out in shock.

"We were ordered to take all of them to be killed."

"You killed those small babies? Oh God!"

My words dried up. His last statement was not a lie. All these years, in the back of my mind, I had always thought that they had spared the children. When visitors saw that particular painting, they used to ask me where the children were taken. I told them that I didn't know but that they might have been taken to an orphanage outside the prison.

On this day in 1996 everything became clear to me. This word "brutal" was too mild to describe their cruelty. I didn't have the courage to ask him how he killed those children and how many of them they had killed. I looked at the room on the top floor of Building C, feeling that the horror was still going on in front of me. The screams of pain of the mothers was mixed with the cries of the babies, making it sound so horrifying.

With unsteady steps I walked very slowly away from Huy and sat down in the painting room. The rest of the day I couldn't concentrate on my work at all. I thought about the meeting with Huy all the way home. The impact on my heart could hardly be coped with. The whole encounter had a feeling of unreality.

Keeping the Memory Alive

Twenty-three years after the Khmer Rouge came to power, on April 17, 1998, I learned that Pol Pot had died. The news came to me abruptly and unexpectedly when a Japanese television crew showed up at my house and asked to interview me at Tuol Sleng.

"Pol Pot is dead," the reporter told me as we stood in the museum surrounded by photographs of the prison's victims. "How do you feel?"

I felt shocked and confused, and tried to confirm the news with the interpreter.

"What? Pol Pot is dead?"

"Yes. He died night before last – what do you think?" the interpreter asked.

I was flooded with a jumble of confused thoughts and emotions. We'd had false alarms before that Pol Pot had died, and at first I did not trust the news. What a coincidence, I thought, if this really is true. A few days earlier I had heard that the United States government was planning to arrest Pol Pot and try him before an international court.

Once the news began to sink in I felt a mixture of sorrow and relief. I was glad that Pol Pot was dead because now Cambodians throughout the world, including myself, knew clearly that the bloodiest master criminal had disappeared forever from this world. There really must be karma, I thought. Here was the man who had held supreme power in Cambodia, whose followers had respected him like a god, and now he had died virtually alone in the middle of the quiet jungle. His body was wrapped in a tarp and burned like an animal. There were no monks there to bless him.

At the same time I felt intense sorrow. I realized that I would never fulfill my long-held desire to see Pol Pot standing in the dock, facing a court to answer for his crimes. How would he have appeared, standing before the tribunal – would he be smiling confidently or trembling and pale? Would he offer any excuses or alibis, or would he confess? But now none of that would happen.

Pol Pot – whom the Cambodian people had feared for more than two decades – had vanished from the world, leaving behind terrible, painful memories and a vicious reputation that would linger in the hearts of every Cambodian.

Nowadays from time to time there is talk of closing the Tuol Sleng Museum of Genocide. There are those who argue that this will help heal the wounds and bring our fractured nation back together. However, I feel very strongly that the museum should stay open. More than 14,000 prisoners were executed at S-21. If Tuol Sleng Museum is abandoned or converted to another purpose, it means that those men, women, and children who died there were simply eliminated; that their deaths were meaningless. I want to keep the memory alive so foreign visitors and the new generation of Cambodians can understand what happened during that time. Our children must learn never to treat human beings like animals, or lower than animals.

If I had ever met Pol Pot or any of his top henchmen I wouldn't have had anything to say to them. They were the top — the chiefs of them all — and far away from me. I never had any direct contact with them or saw their activities with my own eyes.

But it has been different when I've met the guards who worked at Tuol Sleng. If I had met Huy right after escaping from Tuol Sleng I don't know what I would have done. However, when I saw him much later, I felt sorry for him. Instead of a proud torturer, he was a poor farmer living in fear, and I could not raise my hand to kill him. However I feel that he and the top Khmer Rouge leaders should all be punished for the crimes they committed.

It was unbelievable to me when I heard that not long before his death, Pol Pot refused to admit his crimes or apologize to the Cambodian people. Even if he did not commit each murder with his own hands, he should have taken responsibility for his subordinates, the people who answered to him.

Pol Pot died unpunished, without ever having to answer for his deeds. And perhaps the surviving Khmer Rouge leaders will never be punished either. But one way or another, I believe there will be justice. A person harvests what he has sown. According to the Buddhist religion, good actions produce good results, bad actions produce bad results. The peasant harvests the rice, the fisherman catches the fish. Pol Pot and his henchmen will harvest the actions they committed. They will reap what they have sown.